First World War
and Army of Occupation
War Diary
France, Belgium and Germany

14 DIVISION
Divisional Troops
62 Field Company Royal Engineers
20 May 1915 - 16 June 1919

WO95/1889/2

The Naval & Military Press Ltd
www.nmarchive.com
Published in association with The National Archives

Published by

The Naval & Military Press Ltd

Unit 10 Ridgewood Industrial Park,

Uckfield, East Sussex,

TN22 5QE England

Tel: +44 (0) 1825 749494

www.naval-military-press.com

www.nmarchive.com

This diary has been reprinted in facsimile from the original. Any imperfections are inevitably reproduced and the quality may fall short of modern type and cartographic standards.

© **Crown Copyright**
Images reproduced by permission of The National Archives, London, England, 2015.

Contents

Document type	Place/Title	Date From	Date To
Heading	WO/1889/2		
Heading	14th Division 62nd Field Coy. R.E. May 1915-Jun 1919		
Heading	14th Division 62nd Field Coy. R.E. Vol 1. Vol To May To Sept 15 June 19		
Heading	War Diary Of 62 Field Company Royal Engineers From. 20th May. 1915 To. 30th September 1915 Volume 1		
War Diary	Aldershot Southampton Havre Cassel	20/05/1915	27/05/1915
War Diary	St. Sylvestre	28/05/1915	28/05/1915
War Diary	Vlamertinghe	29/05/1915	04/06/1915
War Diary	Vlamertinghe La Clyte	05/06/1915	13/06/1915
War Diary	La Clyte Vlamertinghe	14/06/1915	15/06/1915
War Diary	Ypres	16/06/1915	16/06/1915
War Diary	Vlamertinghe	17/06/1915	08/07/1915
War Diary	H 17 B 7.5	25/07/1915	30/07/1915
Map	Supporting Point R. 3		
Map	Supporting Point R. 4		
Map	Supporting Point R. 7		
Map	Supporting Point R. 5		
Map	Supporting Point R. 8		
War Diary	H, 17 B, 7.5	31/07/1915	06/09/1915
Map	Supporting Point P. 2		
Map			
War Diary	H, 17 B 7.5	07/09/1915	01/10/1915
Map			
Heading	14th Division 62nd F.C.R.E. Vol 2 Oct. 15		
Heading	War Diary Of 62nd Fld Coy Royal Engineers. From 1.10.15 To 31.10.15 Volume 2		
War Diary	H 7a. 6.6	01/10/1915	31/10/1915
Heading	History Of Operations		
Miscellaneous			
Miscellaneous	Possible ?? rests used	20/10/1915	20/10/1915
Diagram etc		20/10/1915	20/10/1915
Heading	14th Division 62nd F.C.R.E. Vol: 3 Nov 15 To Dec		
War Diary	H.7 A. 6.6	01/11/1915	16/12/1915
War Diary	H 7 B 6.6	17/12/1915	10/01/1916
Map	Drains Trenches		
Heading	62nd F.C.R.E. Vol: 5 17/12/15-31/1/16		
War Diary	H 7 B 6.6	10/01/1916	31/01/1916
War Diary	H 7 B 6.6	22/01/1916	31/01/1916
Map			
Heading	62nd F.C.R.E. 14th Div Vol 6		
War Diary	H 7 B 6.6	01/02/1916	12/02/1916
War Diary	Herzeele	12/02/1916	08/03/1916
War Diary	Dainville	08/03/1916	31/03/1916
Diagram etc	R.E. Baths		
War Diary	Dainville	01/04/1916	30/04/1916
Diagram etc	Dressing Station		
Diagram etc	M.G. Emplacement Chateau Ronville		

Type	Description	From	To
Diagram etc	M.G. Emplacement In H.S. Line		
Diagram etc	M.G. Emplacement Achicourt		
War Diary	Dainville	01/05/1916	31/05/1916
Miscellaneous	D.A.G. G.H.Q. 3rd Echelon		
War Diary	Dainville	07/06/1916	30/06/1916
Heading	62 F.C.R.E. App To Vol 10 June		
Miscellaneous	D.A.G GHQ 3rd Echelon	16/07/1916	16/07/1916
Diagram etc	Lewis Gap. Emplacements. At H 30		
Diagram etc	M.G. Emplacement		
Diagram etc	M.G. Emplacement. In H. 40		
Diagram etc	M.G. Emplacement. In Havannah		
War Diary	Dainville	09/07/1916	31/07/1916
Diagram etc	Detail of Iron Cover scale I inch-I foot		
Diagram etc	Sketch Of Turn Table For 18 Fir		
Heading	14th Division. 62nd Field Company Royal Engineers August 1916		
Miscellaneous	C.R.E 14th Divn	19/08/1916	19/08/1916
Diagram etc	Barricade Made By Infantry And Cleaned By Capt Maxwell		
Diagram etc	Diana Work		
Diagram etc			
War Diary		01/08/1916	21/08/1916
War Diary	In The Field	22/08/1916	30/08/1916
War Diary	Dernancourt	31/08/1916	30/09/1916
War Diary	In The Field	01/10/1916	31/10/1916
Heading	War Diary Of 62 F.C.R.E. From 1st November 1916 To 30th November 1916 Volume 1		
War Diary	In The Field	01/11/1916	31/05/1917
Miscellaneous	14th Division "A"	04/07/1917	04/07/1917
War Diary	In The Field	01/06/1917	31/10/1917
War Diary	Dickebusch	01/11/1917	09/11/1917
War Diary	Vlamertinghe	10/11/1917	12/11/1917
War Diary	Potijze	13/11/1917	02/12/1917
War Diary	Ypres Canal Bank	03/12/1917	31/12/1917
War Diary	Ypres	01/01/1918	13/01/1918
War Diary	Eclusier	14/01/1918	21/01/1918
War Diary	Vrely	22/01/1918	22/01/1918
War Diary	Becquigny	23/01/1918	24/01/1918
War Diary	Beines	25/01/1918	26/01/1918
War Diary	Benay	27/01/1918	28/02/1918
Heading	14th Divisional Engineers 62nd Field Company R.E March 1918		
War Diary	Benay	01/03/1918	21/03/1918
War Diary	Jussy Detroit Sammons	22/03/1918	22/03/1918
War Diary	Les Riez De Cugny	22/03/1918	22/03/1918
War Diary	Les Riez De Cogny Montalimont Fm Beaumont En Being Guivry	23/03/1918	23/03/1918
War Diary	Muirancourt	24/03/1918	24/03/1918
War Diary	Muirancourt Lassigny	24/03/1918	24/03/1918
War Diary	Ressons	25/03/1918	25/03/1918
War Diary	Ressons Braisnes	26/03/1918	26/03/1918
War Diary	Braisnes Moyvillers	27/03/1918	27/03/1918
War Diary	Moyvillers Beaurepaire	28/03/1918	28/03/1918
War Diary	Beaurepaire Nogent	29/03/1918	29/03/1918
War Diary	Nogent Bazincourt	30/03/1918	30/03/1918
War Diary	Bazincourt Flechy	31/03/1918	31/03/1918

Miscellaneous	Detailed Account Of Action Of Company On 23rd & 24th March 1918		
Miscellaneous	Copy Of Order Received From G.O.C. 36th Divn. At Bethencourt At 8.50 a.m On 24/3/18	24/03/1918	24/03/1918
Heading	14th Div. 62nd Field Company R.E. April 1918		
War Diary	Vellenes Flechy	01/04/1918	01/04/1918
War Diary	Flechy Vers	02/04/1918	02/04/1918
War Diary	Vers Aubigny	03/04/1918	05/04/1918
War Diary	Blangy	06/04/1918	08/04/1918
War Diary	Amiens	09/04/1918	09/04/1918
War Diary	Monchaux	10/04/1918	11/04/1918
War Diary	Citerne	12/04/1918	12/04/1918
War Diary	Foret De Vignacourt	13/04/1918	14/04/1918
War Diary	Ecquedecques	15/04/1918	15/05/1918
War Diary	Ham-en-Artois	19/05/1918	31/05/1918
War Diary	Ecquedecques	01/06/1918	01/07/1918
War Diary	Clairmarais Forest	09/07/1918	09/07/1918
War Diary	St Sylvestre Cappel	12/07/1918	31/07/1918
War Diary		29/07/1918	29/07/1918
War Diary	St Sylvestre Cappel	01/08/1918	11/08/1918
War Diary	St. Momelin	12/08/1918	12/08/1918
War Diary	Ouest Mont (Eperlecques)	13/08/1918	18/08/1918
War Diary	Louches	19/08/1918	22/08/1918
War Diary	Proven	23/08/1918	23/08/1918
War Diary	Ypres	28/08/1918	12/09/1918
War Diary	Dirty Bucket Area	17/09/1918	18/09/1918
War Diary	Dickebusch Area	19/09/1918	01/10/1918
War Diary	Wytschaete	01/10/1918	02/10/1918
War Diary	Wulverghem	03/10/1918	15/10/1918
War Diary	Smlors Crossing	16/10/1918	18/10/1918
War Diary	Le Blanc Four	19/10/1918	19/10/1918
War Diary	Muscron	20/10/1918	20/10/1918
War Diary	Evregnies	21/10/1918	23/10/1918
War Diary	Dottignies	24/10/1918	26/10/1918
War Diary	Estaimpuis	27/10/1918	14/11/1918
War Diary	La Madeleine (Lille)	15/11/1918	30/11/1918
War Diary	La Madeleine Sh 36k21d5.7	01/12/1918	31/12/1918
War Diary	La Madeline Lille Sheet 36k21d5.7	01/01/1919	20/01/1919
War Diary	La Madeline Lille	21/01/1919	31/01/1919
War Diary	La Madeleine Lille Sheet 36 K 21 D 5.7	01/02/1919	09/02/1919
War Diary	La Madeleine Lille	10/02/1919	08/03/1919
War Diary	Herseaux (Belgium)	09/03/1919	30/04/1919
Miscellaneous	42nd Inf Bde Group	02/06/1919	02/06/1919
War Diary	Herseaux (Belgium)	01/05/1919	31/05/1919
War Diary	Herseaux	01/06/1919	16/06/1919

No 1889 2/28/12

14TH DIVISION

62ND FIELD COY. R.E.

MAY 1915 – JUN 1919

121/7198

14th Division

62nd Field Coy. R.E.

Vol. 1.

May to Sept. 15

June '15

CONFIDENTIAL

WAR DIARY

OF

62 FIELD COMPANY
ROYAL ENGINEERS

FROM. 20ᵗʰ MAY. 1915   TO. 30ᵗʰ SEPTEMBER 1915

VOLUME. 1.

WAR DIARY
INTELLIGENCE SUMMARY

Army Form C. 2118.

Place	Date	Hour	Summary of Events and Information	Remarks and references to Appendices
ALDERSHOT	20/5/15		Left RUSHMOOR CAMP 8.0.a.m. Entrained for FARNBOROUGH STATION, 10.20.a.m.	
SOUTHAMPTON	do		Embarked 3.0.p.m.	
HAVRE	22/5/15		Disembarked. 7.0.a.m. Proceeded to N°2 Rest camp. 10.30.a.m.	
do	24/5/15		Left Rest Camp. 11.0.a.m. Entrained 2.30.p.m.	
CASSEL	26/5/15		Train arrived 1.30.p.m. Received orders from 42nd (Inf.) Brigade to proceed to billets at BOLLEZEELE. Left CASSEL (RY STN) 4.0.p.m. - arrived BOLLEZEELE 7.40.p.m. + proceeded billets in four farms, about 58 men + 20 horses in each farm	
do	27/5/15		Marched to SAINT SYLVESTRE, leaving billets 5.0.a.m., arrived BELLENGIER FERME near ST. SYLVESTRE. 11.30.a.m. where whole company billeted.	
ST. SYLVESTRE	28/5/15		Marched 6.45.a.m. to rendezvous on the orders of C.R.E. XIVth Divn at cross roads on STEENVOORDE - POPERINGHE road 2 miles East of STEENVOORDE: thence to billets at VLAMERTINGHE arriving 1.0.pm. whole company billeted at school opposite church.	
VLAMERTINGHE	29/5/15		Company employed in placing in state of defence a series of posts from a point ½ mile East of VLAMERTINGHE on VLAMERTINGHE - YPRES road to in a North-westerly direction. Posts distributed between same:- N°1 Section to south + remainder in succession. N°1 section one large farm. N°2 section two detached posts N°3 section one farm. N°4 Section three small detached posts. Hdqrs section loading + distributing material	
do	30/5/15		Work continued. but Hdqrs section assisting N°1 Section	
do	31/5/15		Work continued.	
do	1/6/15		Work continued.	
do	2/6/15		Work continued. Chief Engineer General Hiatt inspected works R.E.	
do	3/6/15		Work continued	

R Cullane
Major R.E.
Comdg 62 (2nd) Fd Co R.E.

Army Form C. 2118.

WAR DIARY
or
INTELLIGENCE SUMMARY.
(Erase heading not required.) **62nd Field Coy. R.E.**

Place	Date	Hour	Summary of Events and Information	Remarks and references to Appendices
VLAMERTINGHE	1/6/15	—	Company continued work on line of defended posts, from about ½ mile East of VLAMERTINGHE on VLAMERTINGHE – YPRES road in a N.W. direction. Work continued on points 1, 2, 3, 4 + 6, & commenced on 8 and 9.	
"	2/6/15	—	Work continued: points 10, 11, 12, 13 + 14 commenced. As far as possible completion of M.G. Emp.s + splinter proofs was aimed at while fire + communicating trenches, barbed wire fencing etc. were indicated on the ground firmer by shallow trenches + latter by posts + single strand fence.	
"	3/6/15	—	Work continued.	
"	4/6/15	—	Work continued by small detachments while awaiting orders to move.	
VLAMERTINGHE LA CLYTTE	5/6/15	—	Company marched at 6 a.m. and reached LA CLYTTE at 9.10 a.m., where it went into billets at LA CORNAILLIE FARM about 1m West of LA CLYTTE.	
"	6/6/15	—	At the direction of C.R.E. 14th Divn. by arrangement with C.R.E. 46th Divn. Major Gillam met Major Howard of C.R.E. 46th Divn. at KEMMEL at 9 a.m. and ascertained general requirements for defence of KEMMEL village.	
"	7/6/15	—	Company commenced work on the defences of KEMMEL village, under orders of C.R.E. 46th Divn.	
"	8/6/15	—	" continued	
"	9/6/15	—	" " and commenced repairs + extension to dam on LACLYTTE – KEMMEL road.	
"	10,11,12 16/6/15	—	" "	
"	13/6/15	—	Received orders from C.R.E. + 42nd Inf. Brigade to move to-morrow with 42nd Brigade into F. Corps area.	
LA CLYTTE VLAMERTINGHE	14/6/15	—	Marched at 9.30 a.m. and arrived at point ¾m S.W. of VLAMERTINGHE at 11.35 a.m. Went into billets at Farm H 8 c. 6.2 at 12 noon.	
"	15/6/15	—	At 5.30 p.m. received secret orders for 2 Sections to move eastwards with 42nd Brigade to-night. At 9.45 p.m. 2 Sections (Lieuts. Prescott + Jackson), the whole under Captain Pyfe, marched with 42nd Brigade (Brig. Genl. Markham) in an easterly direction, headquarters and 2 Sections under Major Gillam (with Lt. Barlow) remaining behind at Farm H 8 c. 6.2 in Divl. Reserve under orders of H.Q. 14th Divn.	
YPRES	16/6/15	—	Two Sections remained in trenches until 4.0 p.m. when under orders of G.O.C. 42nd Bde. they followed the 9th Rifle Brigade advancing to support. Major R.A. Gillam R.E. brought forward Nos. 3 + 4 Sections with Lieuts. Crofton + Barlow who took the place of Nos. 1 + 2 Section in trenches + were attached to 41st Inf. Bde. who had now moved up in support of 42nd Inf. Bde. Maj. Gillam + Capt. Pyfe accompanied N°s. 1 + 2 sections to a point about 500 yards S.E. of YPRES ramparts where the battalion commenced to dig itself in under rather heavy shell fire. The section assisted the infantry in their operation but at about 8 p.m.	P.T.O

Army Form C. 2118.

WAR DIARY
or
INTELLIGENCE SUMMARY.
(Erase heading not required.)

Instructions regarding War Diaries and Intelligence Summaries are contained in F.S. Regs., Part II. and the Staff Manual respectively. Title pages will be prepared in manuscript.

Hour, Date, Place		Summary of Events and Information	Remarks and references to Appendices
YPRES.	16/6/15. (continued)	the shelling becoming heavier the whole party retired to WEST of YPRES + at about 10.p.m orders were received for the sections concerned to return to billets. N°s 3+4 sections were ordered to bivouac near KRUISTRADT.	
VLAMERTINGE.	17/6/15.	N°s 1+2 Sections rejoining N°: 3+4 remained in neighbourhood of YPRES with 41st Inf. Bde.	
"	18/6/15.	N°s 3+4 section returned to billets at 9.a.m.	
"	19/6/15.	42nd Inf Bde having moved in relief to occupy 1st line Trenches N.E. of YPRES N°2 section (2/Lt Jackson) went out with them for engineer work, owing to shelling + gas attacks by the enemy very little could be done + the section returned at 4.30.p.m. next morning	
"	20/6/15.	N°s 1+4 sections employed on strengthening + repairing Parapets. bringing up stores etc.	
"	21/6/15.	N°1 section returned 4.30.a.m. N°4 at 12 m.n. N°s 2+3 moved up in relief, + continued work, no stores + in addition some section of trench + obstacles + or saps. Major R.A. Gillam wounded while inspecting	
"	22/6/15	N°s 2+3 returning to estm? (possibly working party) next day some sunk mines. (following day) N°s 1+4 moved up in their neighbourhood.	
"	23/6/15.	Major Gillam sent to Hospital. N°s 2+3 sections returned. N°s 1+4 with Capt. Y.C. R.E. moved up to assist in attack orders for which are attached. Both sections were subjected to heavy bombardment in trenches. N°4 Section (Lieut. Barbin.) accompanied the assaulting columns, but and under orders of O.C. East column advanced to support infantry who were held up. The whole column was forced to retire however + the section regained the trenches with the loss of 7 NCOs + men wounded *. The working party scheme had to be abandoned. N°4 section returned at about 10.a.m. N° 1 remained in trenches until 7.p.m. repairing shattered parapets + working at saps. N°s 2+ 3 moved up in relief + worked at barbed wire obstacles returning early next morning.	* attend by 5th Wor'r + Bucks L.I. dressing station

Army Form C. 2118.

WAR DIARY
or
INTELLIGENCE SUMMARY.
(Erase heading not required.)

Instructions regarding War Diaries and Intelligence Summaries are contained in F. S. Regs., Part II. and the Staff Manual respectively. Title pages will be prepared in manuscript.

Hour, Date, Place	Summary of Events and Information	Remarks and references to Appendices
24/6/15 LAMBERTINGE	No. 2 + 3 sections returned 4.30 a.m. Headquarters of unit moved ½ mile N.W. to escape enemy's shells. Infantry relief night so only Lieuts. Prescott + Barlow + 4 NCOs to trenches to direct relieving Brigade in work to be undertaken, (no work possible on relief nights)	
25/6/15	No. 1 + 2 sections working with infantry working party on communication trenches, returning 4.30 a.m.	
26/6/15	No. 3 + 4 sections as above, returning 4.30 p.m.	
27/6/15	No. 1 + 2 sections on new communication trench work. Orders issued for sections in trenches to remain there in future.	
28/6/15	No. 3 + 4 sections in trenches for 24 hours. New forward communication trench should have been started but owing to artillery bombardment it was decided to complete new communication trench (Y).	
29/6/15	No. 1 + 2 sections. New forward communication trench commenced with 2 coys. 11th Kings (L'pool) Regt. = Good progress made.	
30/6/15	No. 3 + 4 section. New forward comm. trench completed + partly revived old southern to comm. trench between G.H.Q 2 + Rly embankment path. Tumnel filled in a bombed.	
1/7/15	No. 1 + 2 sections. No.1 drying new forward communication trench. No.2 digging out eastern recently revived. No.2 completing rear communications commenced 30/6/15.	

Army Form C. 2118

WAR DIARY
or
INTELLIGENCE SUMMARY.
(Erase heading not required.)

Instructions regarding War Diaries and Intelligence Summaries are contained in F. S. Regs., Part II. and the Staff Manual respectively. Title pages will be prepared in manuscript.

Place	Date	Hour	Summary of Events and Information	Remarks and references to Appendices
VLAMERTINGE	1/7/15	—	Nos 1 & 2 Sections. No.1 with working party draining new forward communication trench & clearing Eastern Assembly trenches. No.2 completing rear communications commenced 30/6/15.	
"	2/7/15	—	Nos 3 & 4 Sections. Carrying parties and bringing up materials to site of new supporting pt. at White Château & fixing sign boards etc.	
"	3/7/15	—	Nos 1 & 2 Sections only to White Château. Constructing splinter proofs.	
"	4/7/15	—	Nos 3 & 4 " with 1 Coy. 11th Kings. L'pool's on communication & fire trenches in White Château. Night work only, possible returned 3.0 am. splinter proof.	
"	5/7/15	—	No. 1 Section to White Château with 100 infantry, fire & commn. trenches. Nos 3 & 4 Sections detailed for day work on retired supporting points. Four points each with 2 daily reliefs of 100 infantry. Working parties 7a.m.–11 a.m. & 5 p.m. to 9 p.m.	
"	6/7/15	—	1st Corps commander (Gen. Sir E. H. Allenby) visited White Château & ordered work to be stopped & a new supporting point commenced about 150 yards to West of it. Old trenches already dug to be filled in. No.2 Section with 200 infantry employed on latter at night.	
"	7/7/15	—	Major MACKESY R.E. & Capt PYE visited new supporting point & to decide form of work required. Decided to construct 3 advanced works & one central work of breastwork type with splinter proofs, all self contained & connected by communication trench. Work S. of MENIN road connected by tunnel under road. No.1 Section with 250 infantry commenced work at night. & worked on new communication trench to No.1 Château grounds. Nos 3 & 4 Sections with 400 infantry commenced work on rear supporting points by day. No.2 Section with 1 Coy infantry continued work on new forward	
"	8/7/15	—	Nos 3 & 4 Sections continued work as above. No.2 Section supporting point by night	

Army Form C. 2118.

WAR DIARY
or
INTELLIGENCE SUMMARY.
(Erase heading not required.)

Instructions regarding War Diaries and Intelligence Summaries are contained in F. S. Regs., Part II. and the Staff Manual respectively. Title pages will be prepared in manuscript.

Place	Date	Hour	Summary of Events and Information	Remarks and references to Appendices
H17B	25/7/15	8 a.m.	Two sections in trenches. Sapps 2a, 2b, proceeded with. 2a stopped owing to wet front in front of 6B3 but made continuous. Inf. knocked off at midnight on account of shelling. Sapps 4a, 6a, 6B3 also proceeded with. About 50 "60" of wire put out in front of 6B3 supporting pts. Work on parapets & dugout in Fairway. 12 knife rests put out in front of 6a.	
	26/7/15	8a.m.	Relief of sections. Sapps 2a, 2b, 4a, 6a, 6B proceeded with. 10 knife rests put out in front of H13 + H14.	
	27/7/15		Reconno. that 9 am afraid. Sapps proceeded + supporting points. Also section of stone trench M.G. emplacement in F9 proceeded at 6 O.R. where the united trenches. Arrangements for stores for same. Section of plate etc., started.	
	28/7/15			
	29/7/15		1 Section Trenches by night. Working trenches + supporting points R1 + R3. new supporting point R4 started. Sap completed. 2 Section by day Trenches. 3 Section on new trunches &. 4 Section on huts.	
	30/7/15	8 a.m.	1 Section by day. M.G. Emplacements (Ste.) 2 Section by night on three supporting points R1, R3, R4. 3 Section making handling + some necessary drainage work in camp. 4 Section transfer of huts & park installation at SAILLY PORT. O.C. visited site of new M.G. Emplacements. G.H.Q. with A.D.S.S./Forms/C. 2118. lack of communication trench with O.C. Pioneers by night	

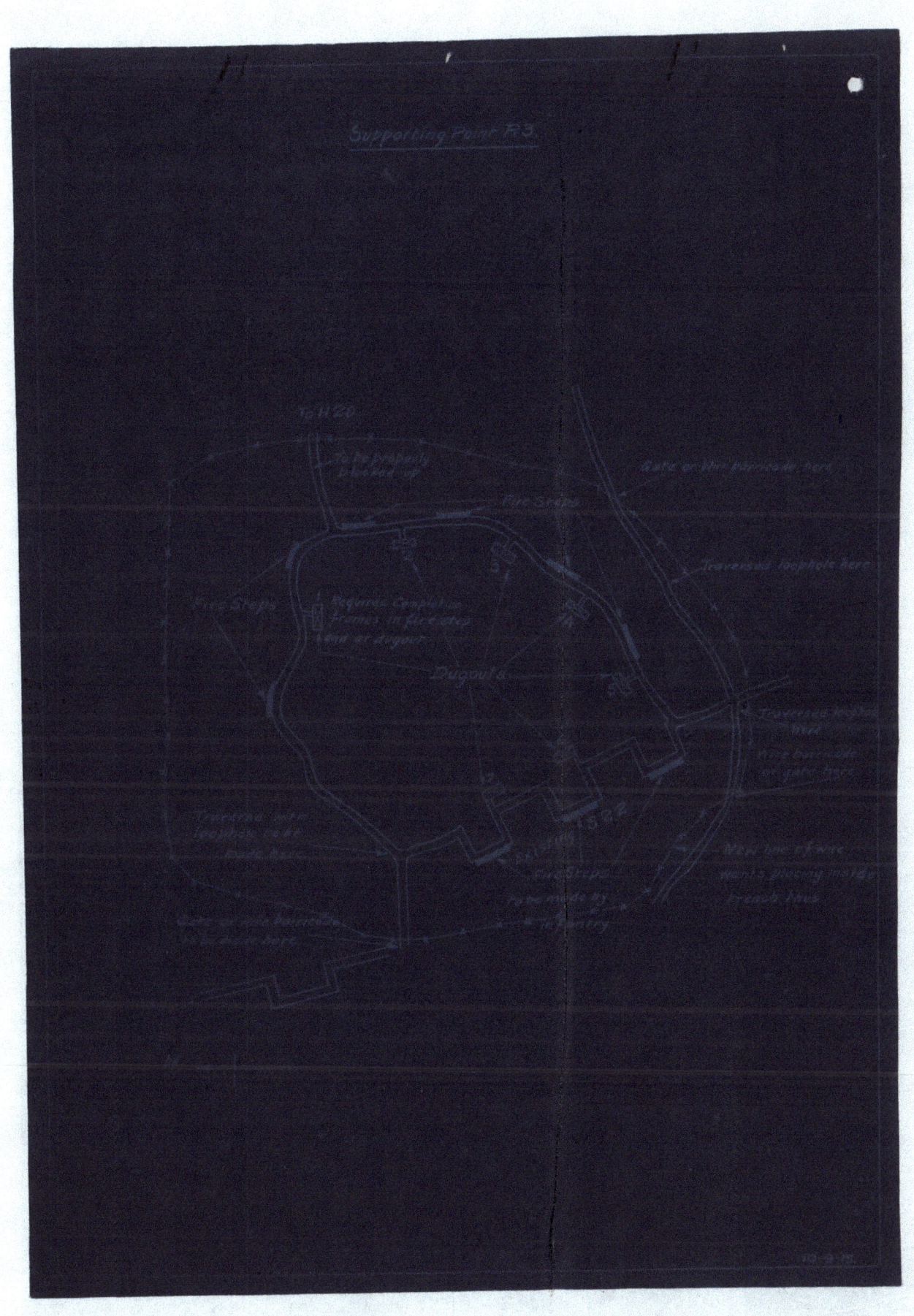

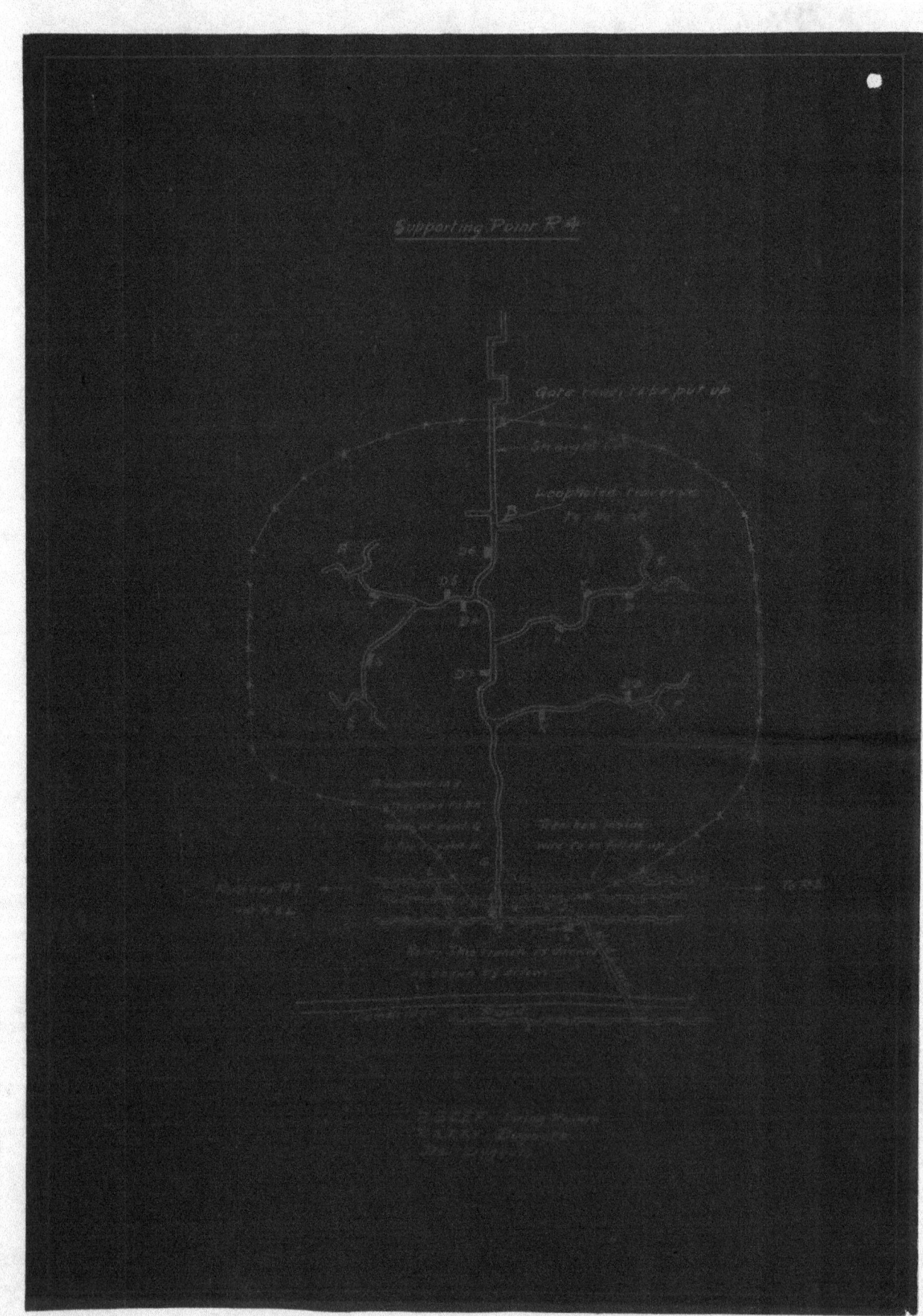

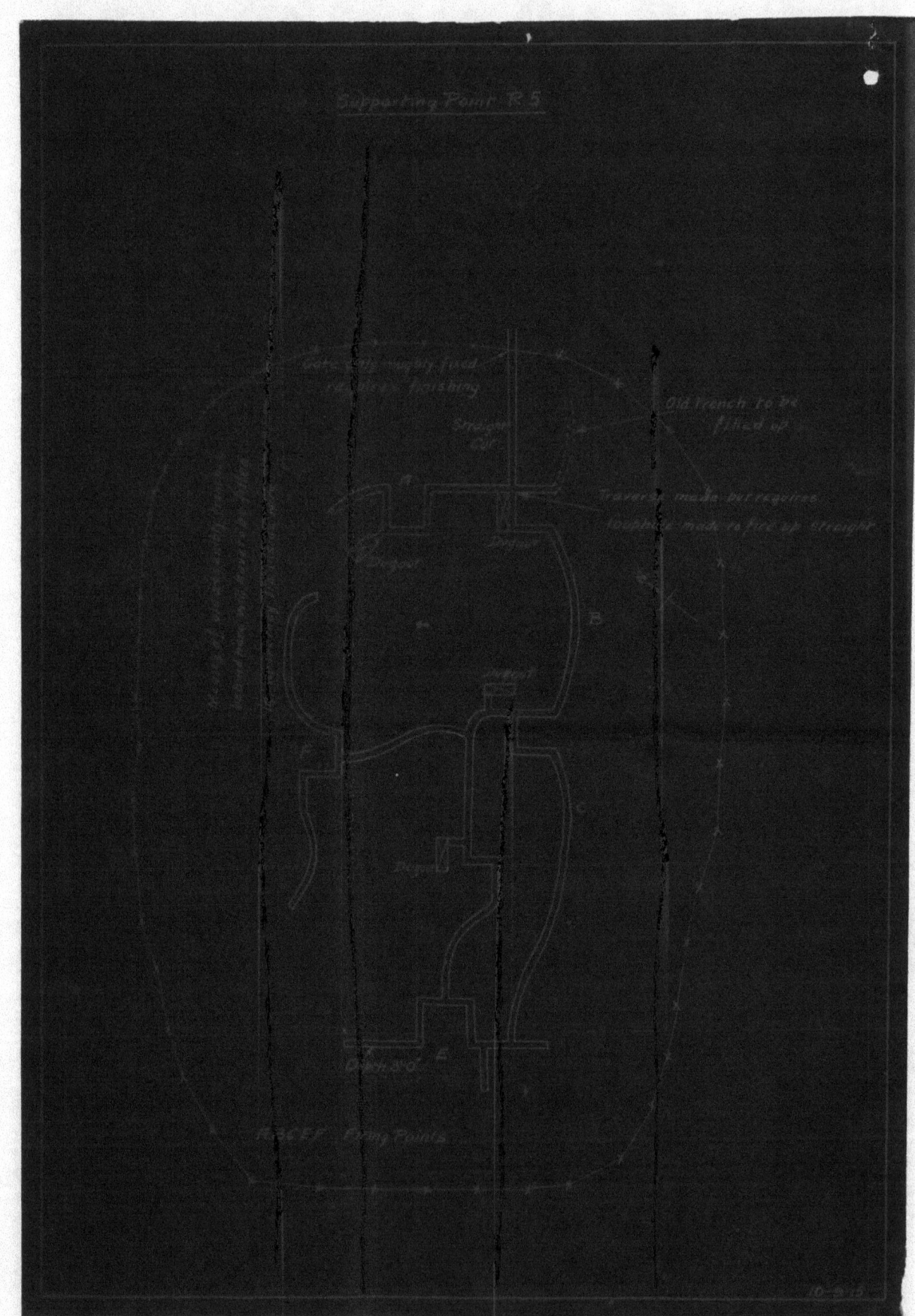

WAR DIARY or INTELLIGENCE SUMMARY

Army Form C. 2118

Instructions regarding War Diaries and Intelligence Summaries are contained in F. S. Regs., Part II. and the Staff Manual respectively. Title pages will be prepared in manuscript.

(Erase heading not required.)

Place	Date	Hour	Summary of Events and Information	Remarks and references to Appendices
H, 7, B, 7, S.	31/7/15	8 a.m.	1 Section marched up to lay cups & M.G. emplacement. 2 Section moved up from Brielen between Km bright sector. 4 Section worked whilst attacked a flank in water at HALF PORT instructors, whilst for it. My been independent all night. Attempts made by 1 section traffic tempts. Others assisted in repairing trenches O.C. at Ste Jdyre. church.	8 softys wounded
	1/8/15	8 a.m.	1 Section staffed proceeding & putting by R.F.A. fires southward. 2 Section in relief after night in trenches. 1/2 rested after night wk. 1/2 wk by night. Break M.G. emplacement for M.G. cats out along during heavy shelling. 4 Section noted doing camp fatigues after 12 hours work. O.C. proceeded VLAMERTINGHE.	22 softys wounded
	2/8/15	8 a.m.	1 Section by day in trenches. 2 Section by night 3 sapps 17, 16 & 22 proceeded with, at Hq stepped any M.T.C. emplacement in trench G.10. 3 Section & an M.G. employed at M.P.2 (trench not do-re) by night any 5 heavy shelling. 1/2 tried to carry material but day - 1/2 by day. 1/2 tried be carry minirab water to YPRES, dig g, save at BRANDHOEK, report communication in G.H.Q. 4 Section emp't at YPRES on night, RA/Saft, NLM meeting he return & emp't on relief. 2 Section returned to camp in evening.	
	3/8/15	8 a.m.	1 Section worked on 3 sapps & M.G. employments. 3 Section M.G. emplacement on G.H.Q. also 3 dag & carry, earning him for some by night. 4 Section repairing trenches 85, 82 & by night.	
	4/8/15	8 a.m.	1 Section worked by night on new arrangmt of trenches. All officers on source. 250 Leicesters 3 Saps proceeded continuously from 3 & 4 Sections	2 killed 2 wounded Leicester (1 softy killed)
	5/8/15	8 a.m.	1 & 2 section rested after night work. 3 & 4 on new branch trenches by night. O.C. went to 41st Div Hdqrs, with 200 Leicesters in accordance with instructions from acting C.R.E. 3 Saps proceeded continuously from 3 & 4 Sections	1 softy wounded
	6/8/15	8 a.m.	1 Section on tools in VLAMERTINGHE. Own interests at YPRES. 1 Section sanitary wk in camp 4 Company employment for M.G. emplacements. 1 Section on sapps that recently trenches. 1 section safe retd. O.C. visited VLAMT. returned LCRE. Returned Rotk hdqrs in evening. 2 Saps proceeded from 3rd Section.	

1577 Wt.W10791/1773 500,000 1/15 D.D.&L. A.D.S.S./Forms/C. 2118.

WAR DIARY
or
INTELLIGENCE SUMMARY.

Army Form C. 2118.

(Erase heading not required.)

Place	Date	Hour	Summary of Events and Information	Remarks and references to Appendices
H.37.B.7.5	7/8/15	8 a.m.	1 Section putting up hut 16m water supply YPRES. 2 Section given M.G. emplacements by day in G.H.Q. 2. 9 men caught in work at night. Repairs camp sanitation. 3 Section Travelling night. Putting up entanglement in front of retrenchment in triangle. 4 Section Trenches by day. Safe 17, 16, 22. M.G. emplacement. O.C. visited MANERTMAKE + had meeting with C.R.E. + other O.C.s. Arranged details for landing new with O.C. Bg H.	
	8/8/15	8 a.m.	1 + 2 sections as above. 3 Section on same work. 4 Section Trenches by day, 3 safes + M.G. emplacement. O.C. inspected M.G. emplacements + saw TUNNEL GUN R column. recconitered railway in vicinity of HELL FIRE CORNER & in	
	9/8/15	8 a.m.	No work possible at WHITE CHATEAU – as working parties allowed out. 3 + 4 sections – no entanglement in retrenchment. 2 section M.G. emplacements.	
	10/8/15	8 a.m.	1 Section WHITE CHATEAU putting up hurdles nightly. 2 Section M.G. emplacements. 3 Section working huts + mine casing. 4 Section as for N° 3.	
	11/8/15	8 a.m.	1 Section + 3 Section WHITE CHATEAU, wiring by night. 2 Section M.G. emplacements. 4 section making huts + mine casing – finishing water supply YPRES.	
	12/8/15	8 a.m.	1 + 3 sections as previous night. 2 Section as previous day. 4 section as previous day.	1 Sec. Cpl. wounded
	13/8/15	8 a.m.	1 + 3 sections do. do. 2 section do. do.	do (died later)
	14/8/15	8 a.m.	1 + 3 sections do. do. 2 section do. do. 4 section in Res. supports. Party sent up to M.G. emplacements. Party 250 from in morning.	1 Sgt. wounded 1 Sap wounded

1577—Wt-W10791/1773 500,000 1/15 D.D.&L. A.D.S.S./Forms/C. 2118.

WAR DIARY or INTELLIGENCE SUMMARY

Army Form C. 2118.

(Erase heading not required.)

Instructions regarding War Diaries and Intelligence Summaries are contained in F. S. Regs., Part II. and the Staff Manual respectively. Title pages will be prepared in manuscript.

Place	Date	Hour	Summary of Events and Information	Remarks and references to Appendices
H 17 & 7.5	15/8/15	6 p.m.	1 & 2 Section WHITE CHATEAU by night working out 2 Section M.G. Emplacements in G.H.Q.2. Rear supporting points. 3 & 4 Section & M.G. Emplacements. 250 reinforcements in morning.	1 Cpl + 1 Dmr injured by shell in YPRES not serious
	16/8/15	6 a.m.	1 Section resting. 3 Section as previous night. 2 & 4 Section as previous day & night.	
	17/8/15	6 a.m.	WHITE CHATEAU by night with (Infantry) 2 Section ½ by day + ½ by night on M.G. Emplacements. 3 Section emplacements. Camp trenches etc, was supporting points, redoubts # 17A + # 10.D. 1 Section new supporting points 4 Section.	
	18/8/15	8 a.m.	WHITE CHATEAU an infantry had night shelling etc, 1 Section Camp trenches etc, new supporting 3 Section M.G. Emplacements G.H.Q.2. ½ by day + ½ by night. 4 Section points 2 Section	
	19/8/15	8 a.m.	WHITE CHATEAU – 250 Infantry. 2 Section M.G. Emplacements G.H.Q.2. ½ by day + ½ by night new supporting points 1 Section camp trenches etc, 4 Section R3 continued in support line 3 Section as supporting.	
	20/8/15	8 a.m.	R4 continued in support line – wiring etc, 2 Section camp trenches etc, 3 Section as above. trenches etc, wiring, dug outs etc, M.G. dugout. 1 Section R4 continued. 4 Section 2 Section R3 continued.	
	21/8/15	8 a.m.	1 Section Supporting points. 25 drafts R4, + R5. 4 section R3 + M.G. dug out prepared ready for cementing. 2 Section	
	22/8/15	8 a.m.	1 Section preparing stone ready for front. 3 Section Rear supporting Points. M.G. dug outs + Camp Emplacements.	

1577 Wt. W10791/1773 500,000 1/15 D. D. & L. A.D.S.S./Forms/C. 2118.

WAR DIARY
or
INTELLIGENCE SUMMARY.
(Erase heading not required.)

Army Form C. 2118.

Instructions regarding War Diaries and Intelligence Summaries are contained in F. S. Regs., Part II. and the Staff Manual respectively. Title pages will be prepared in manuscript.

Place	Date	Hour	Summary of Events and Information	Remarks and references to Appendices
H.17.B. 7/5	23/8/15	8 a.m.	2 Section R3 & R8 supporting points in support line. wiring & dug outs. 3 Section R4 & R5 as for N°2. 1 Section Camp. Dug out frames etc., 4 Section Rear supporting points. Dug out frames & M.G. Emplacements.	Capt. Hingston reported for duty.
	24/8/15	8 a.m.	2 Section R3 supporting point. wiring & dug outs. Concrete roof to M.G. dug out completed. 3 Section R4. wiring & dug outs. 1 Section camp. dug out frames etc., 4 Section rear supporting points. dug out frames & M.G. Emplacements.	O.C. proceeded home on leave.
	25/8/15	8 a.m.	2 Section R3. new M.G. dug out started. 3 Section R5. 1 Section in camp. dug out frames etc., 4 Section at R.E. Park. making brick road etc.,	
	26/8/15	8 a.m.	2 section R3. & M.G. dug out. 3 Section R4 & R5. 1 Section in camp. frames etc., 4 Section R.E. Park. brick road.	
	27/8/15	8 a.m.	2 Section R3 & M.G. dug out. 2 sappers doing wiring with garrison in front. 3 Section 75 Infy. 1 Section camp dug out frames. 4 Section collecting timber in V.C.17 & R.E. Park.	
	28/8/15	8 a.m.	2 Section R3. 50 Infy. 3 Section R4 & R5. 50 Infy. 1 Section camp. 4 Section R.E. Park.	O.C. returned from leave.
	29/8/15	8 a.m.	1 Section R4 & R5. 4 Section R3 & M.G. dug out. 2 & 3 Sections ½ day work in camp.	

Army Form C. 2118

WAR DIARY
or
INTELLIGENCE SUMMARY.
(Erase heading not required.)

Instructions regarding War Diaries and Intelligence Summaries are contained in F. S. Regs., Part II. and the Staff Manual respectively. Title pages will be prepared in manuscript.

Place	Date	Hour	Summary of Events and Information	Remarks and references to Appendices
Ref. 8.75	30/8/15	8 a.m.	1 Section R₄ + R₅. mixing + dug outs. 4 Section R₃ moving + dug outs + M.G. dug out. 2 Section R.E. Park + N.L.A.M. getting bricks + laying the Park road. 3 Section Camp. dug out frames.	
	31/8/15	8 a.m.	1 Section R₄ + R₅ + 75 Infty. 4 Section 75 Infty. R₃ + R₈ 2+3 Section above + flag for topping up of fortification. as above. 3 Section hutts to men 87½ began showground.	
	1/9/15	8 a.m.	1 Section R₄ + R₅. 75 Infty. 4 Section as above. 2+3 Section as above.	
	2/9/15	8 a.m.	1 Section R₃ + R₈ 70 Infty. 3 Section R₁₁ + R₅ 65 Infty. 1 Section Camp. ½ day frames etc.	
	3/9/15	8 a.m.	2 Section no work neither to-lad —do— 3 Section Re. Park + N.L.A.M. & Section showground + horse lines in camp.	
	4/9/15	8 a.m.	2 + 3 Section no work recommenced swing train. 1 Section R.E. Park + N.L.A.M. 4 Section showground + camp.	
	5/9/15	8 a.m.	1 Section ½ day Park ½ day at P, preparing for inspection coming next day. 4 Section showground + preparing frames to font. 2 Section to work. Police causualty from train from POPERINGHE around was too bad for any work the done. 3 Section a little work at R.S.	Capt. Morgan proceeded on leave.
	6/9/15	8 a.m.	2 Section as Inft. R₃ + R₈ mixing + dug outs & rushing up work destroyed by rain. 1 Section P, work. 4 Section camp + showground + frames for font. 3 Section do Infty. do R₄ + R₅.	

1577 Wt. W10791/1773 500,000 7/15 D. D. & L.   A.D.S.S./Forms/C. 2118.

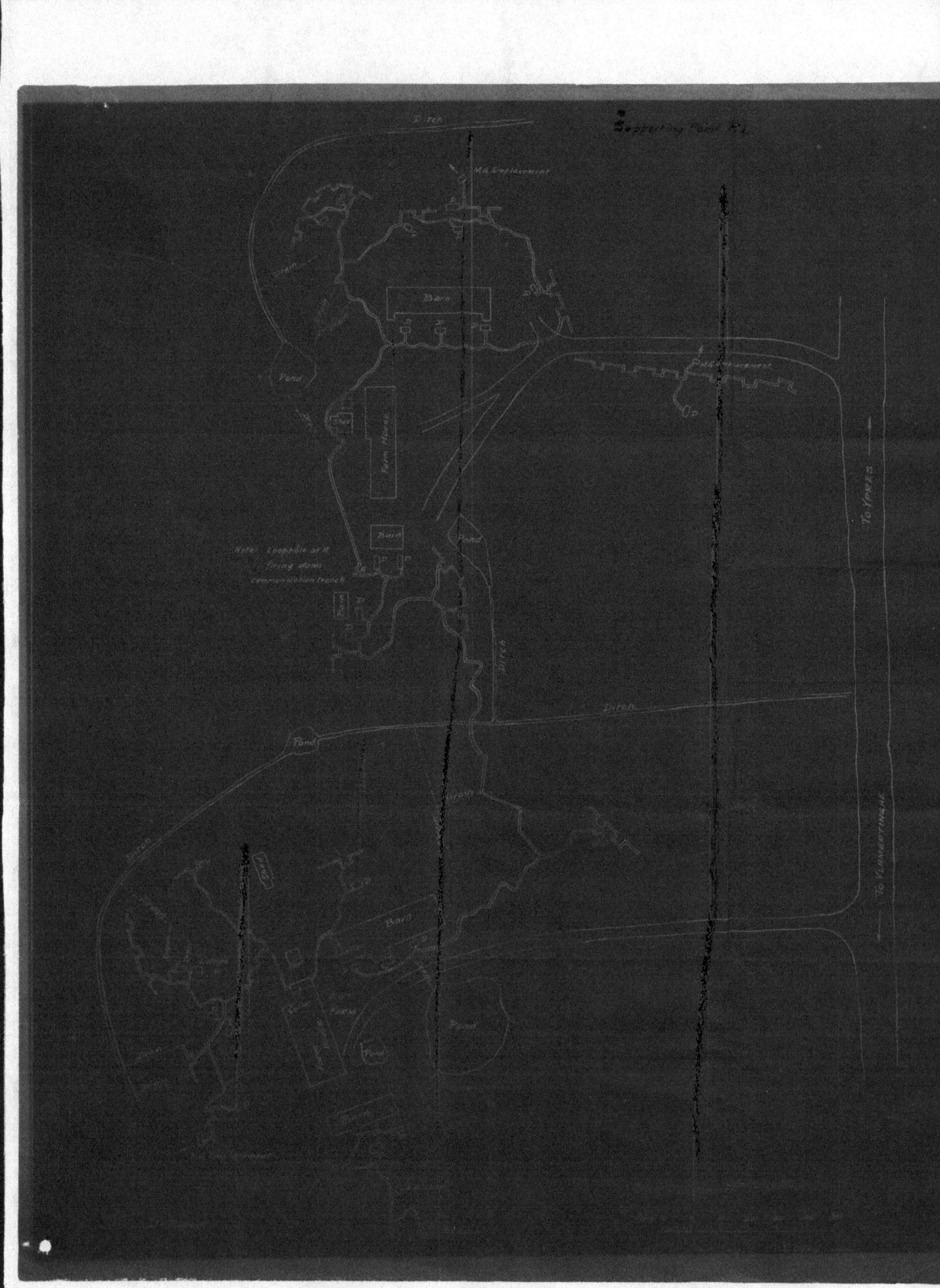

WAR DIARY
or
INTELLIGENCE SUMMARY
(Erase heading not required.)

Army Form C. 2118.

Place	Date	Hour	Summary of Events and Information	Remarks and references to Appendices
H.17.B.7.5	7/9/15	8 a.m.	2 Section R3 + R8, 70 Infy. 3 Section R4 + R5, 70 Infy. 4 Section camp work. 1 Station. P, work.	
	8/9/15	8 a.m.	2 Section R3 + R8 irrig. & dug out. 3 Section R4 + R5. 1 Station P, work no infantry. 4 Section camp work. Finished camp show ground for time being.	
	9/9/15	8 a.m.	2 Section R8 irrig. & trench work. Jule dug out previously noted at sec done. 3 Section R4 + R5 finishing trenches. 1 Section P, 200 Infy. 4 Section camp work. R4 too 11 dug outs irrig. a straight cuts done. R5, 3 dug out, irrig. restraight cuts. R3, 6 dug outs trenching. R8 irrig. no dug out.	
	10/9/15	8 a.m.	1 Section commenced 4 dug outs on AID POST in HENIN ROAD. tunnelling & dug outs finish a station in S18. M.G. dug out in A17 A line. 4 Section 4 dug out in RAILWAY EMBANKMENT & 1 dug out in S. in RAILWAY WOOD. 1 dug out in RAILWAY at 14.2a. 2 Section ½ day after return from front line.	
	11/9/15	8 a.m.	1 Section dug outs HENIN ROAD, position of the two dug outs changed 6 A16. 4 Section dug outs RAILWAY EMBANKMENT. dug out at A72 done. M.G. dug out in hand. 2 Section P2 200 Infy in afternoon. 3 Section P1 200 Infy in afternoon.	

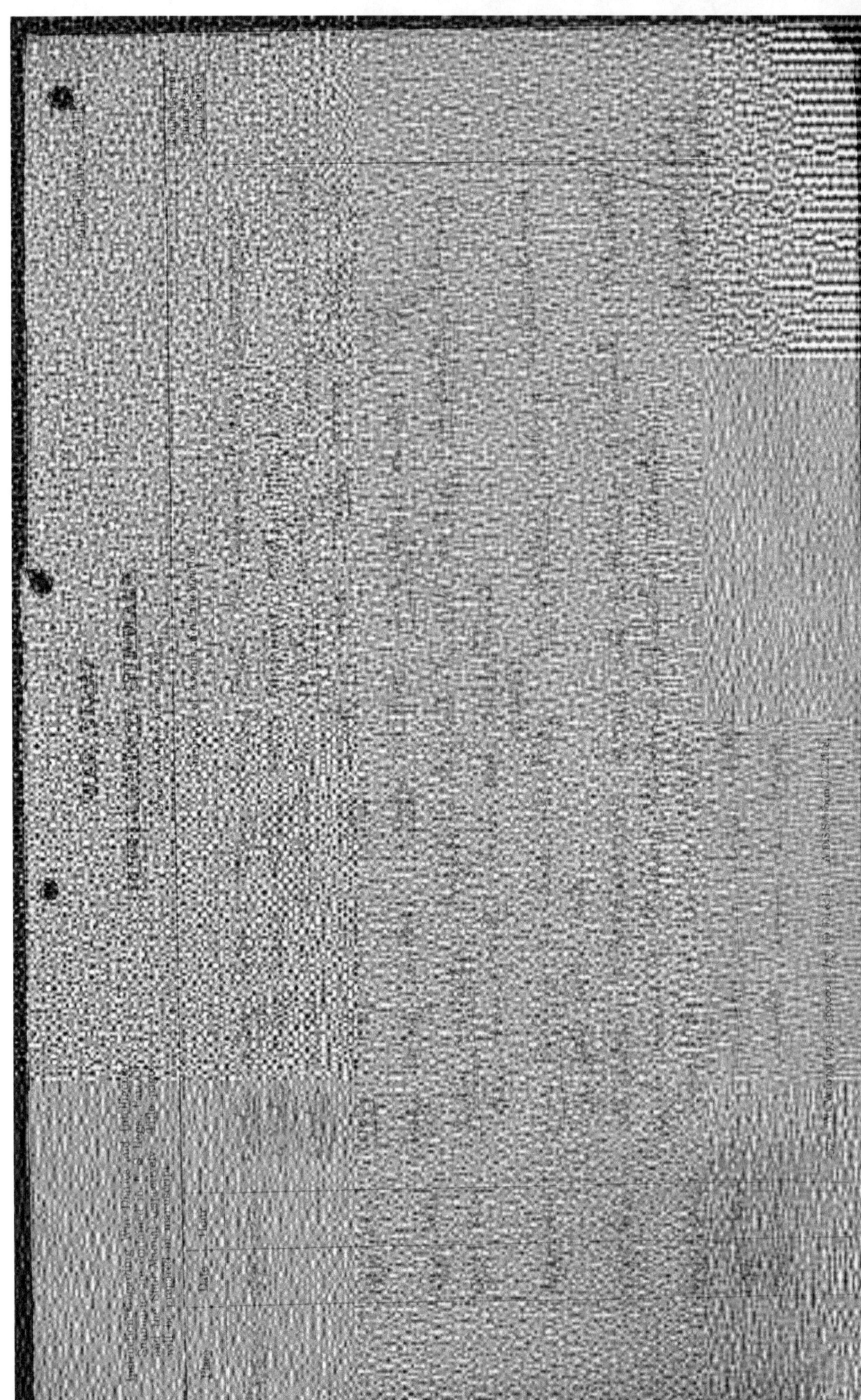

WAR DIARY
or
INTELLIGENCE SUMMARY.

Army Form C. 2118.

Place	Date	Hour	Summary of Events and Information	Remarks and references to Appendices
A.7.B.7.S.	24/9/15	8 a.m.	Ashford. See attached report on operations marked "A."	Casualties Officers wounded 2 O.R. Killed 9 O.R. wounded 14
	26 to 27/9/15		Returned to camp.	
	27/9/15	8 a.m.	Relieved by 85th Coy R.E.	
	28/9/15	8 a.m.	Rested. Nº 2 + 4 worked on camp duties.	
	29/9/15	8 a.m.	Nos 1, 3, + 4 sections worked in camp on various duties. Workshop, hygiene room, showground. Nº 2 Section commenced work on hutting.	
	30/9/15	8 a.m.	Nº 2 Section now permanently placed on hutting. Nºs 1 + 3 Sections commencing repair handling trestles. No 4 Section in camp. By night work on WHITE CHATEAU. Workshop + drainage of camp.	
	1/10/15	8 a.m.	½ day working in camp.	

1/10/15

C.H.R. Chavasse
Capt.
O.C. 6th Coy R.E.

121/7518

14th Hussein

62nd F.C.R.E.
Vol 2

Oct 15

K

CONFIDENTIAL.

War Diary

of

62nd Fld. Coy Royal Engineers.

from. 1:10:15   to 31:10:15.

Volume 2.

WAR DIARY
or
INTELLIGENCE SUMMARY.
(Erase heading not required.)

Army Form C. 2

Instructions regarding War Diaries and Intelligence Summaries are contained in F.S. Regs., Part II. and the Staff Manual respectively. Title pages will be prepared in manuscript.

Place	Date	Hour	Summary of Events and Information	Remarks and references to Appendices
3rd Fd Coy H.Q.	1/10/15	2 a.m.	No 2 Section Hutting. No 1 Section WHITE CHATEAU. No 3 Section WHITE CHATEAU, repairing handle rail bridge 250 left. No 4 f section work in camp. work resturfaced. Which had fallen down owing to undermining of rain & cutting new communication trench.	
	2/10/15	—	No 2 as above. No 1 WHITE CHATEAU. 150 Inf. cutting new communication trenches. No 3 work out of KAAIE SALIENT bequit Brigadier for work on Front line. No 4 in camp on repair.	
	3/10/15	—	No 1 — as above — with 150 Inf.ys. No 2 at disposal R.E.C. 41st Bde. No 4 on do	
	4/10/15	—	Bomb — No 1 & 3 at disposal R.E.C. 41st Duty. Bde for work on Front line. No 4 as above.	
	5/10/15	—	all same as above. ← 14 reinforcements arrived.	
	6/10/15	—	do	
	7/10/15	—	do — begun making stone troughs as well as ordinary trench shores.	
	8/10/15	—	Show-ground, drying rooms workshop completed.	
	9/10/15 10/10/15 11/10/15	—	as above. Horse troughs in camp, dugs, gutters and underground. Horses watering place drunk on picket lines.	

Army Form C. 2118.

WAR DIARY
or
INTELLIGENCE SUMMARY.
(Erase heading not required.)

Instructions regarding War Diaries and Intelligence Summaries are contained in F. S. Regs., Part II. and the Staff Manual respectively. Title pages will be prepared in manuscript.

Place	Date	Hour	Summary of Events and Information	Remarks and references to Appendices
Ypres No A 66	12/10/15	8 a.m.	No 4 Section to front line in lieu of No 1 Section. No 3 with Bgde. 41st Brigade in Trenches Battalion	
	13/10/15	8 a.m.	No 1 Section BEKAARE SALIENT to work with & supported 2 companies Infantry. 3 men in front line. No 2 Hutting.	
	14/10/15	6 a.m.	OR. 6 Trench line of 41st Brigade have gone in trenches. No 3 Section returned to camp. No 1 KKAARE SALIENT & BEKAARE works. No 2 as before.	
	15/10/15	—	OC Res on section of each Coy. Under him in front line. No 3 Section again brought up to front line being temporary arise from Germans blowing up a mine.	
	16/10/15			
	17/10/15			
	18/10/15		Front line work special report attached. Brigade work continued in detail. S.18 trench was repaired & put in order, wiring in front done, wiring road R3 + R2, R4 all done. Dugouts near Fort F6 + C.T. trench with dam drawn. Drainage along upper end CAMBRIDGE ROAD etc.,	On 20/10/15 1st Pte Gridley etc. killed
	19/10/15			
	20/10/15			
	21/10/15			
	22/10/15		returned to camp for Divisional Rest.	
	23/10/15			
	24/10/15		To — temporary Camp for winter. (Putting up shells, trenches sloping etc.)	
	25/10/15			
	26/10/15			

Army Form C. 211

WAR DIARY
or
INTELLIGENCE SUMMARY.
(Erase heading not required.)

Place	Date	Hour	Summary of Events and Information	Remarks and references to Appendices
H.Q. F.1	27/10/15	6 a.m.	No. 2 Section Hutting in Rest area.	
	28/10/15	6 a.m.	No. 1, 3 & 4 Sections Preparing camp for winter; two new huts erected, paths laid out, stoves erected, glimaces(?) from made good.	
	29/10/15	6 a.m.		
	30/10/15	6 a.m.	Capt. Morgan R.E. + 2 N.C.O's detached for work on Brigade Trench show	
	31/10/15	6 a.m.	ground.	

History of Operations

__Night 17/18.__ S20 opened up from D to C,
length along trench about 150 yds
depth about 3 ft, width about 2'.
Considerable delay in starting owing to having
to reconnoitre the position in the dark.

Officer who said he knew line
of trench could of course not find it as it
was all covered in.
Trench was opened up but could only be
made by a man walking very carefully.

__South bombing trench__, 25 yards long.

At beginning of work, this bombing post
was only about 9 ft away from G.
G B was made about 4 ft 6" deep & 2' wide.
T head cut at end into crater & a loophole
placed overlooking East side of crater.

__North Bombing trench__ About 75 yds long

More delay was caused reconnoitring.
Bombing post at beginning of night was
about 15 feet up from G at the old mine
shaft.
We started sapping northwards but after

an hour we decided to dig in the open & a working party was obtained at once from O.C. Oxf & Bucks.

I extended to A as far as I thought I could get in the night & from which I considered we could control the craters properly.

Trench was cut about 3' deep & 2' wide. Difficult work as there were many trees & obstructions.

A complaint was made that this trench was not traversed at the beginning. Considering that we laid out & dug a trench sticking straight out towards the Germans all we could do was to get straight ahead as fast as we could. There was no time to look in.

<u>Wiring</u>   In front of S20. From 11 to S20 single line French wire. About 75 x.

<u>Establishing the bombing Post.</u>   From P round south bombing Post <u>one</u> row knife rests.

From M round north bombing Post <u>one</u> row knife rests.

Night. 18/19

S.20.   Improving — Traverses, sandbagging
        deepening & widening.
        Work poor as parties were very tired.
        Some trees were cut.

G.B.   Completed to 7'6" deep about & trees
        cut.

G.A.   Deepened & widened. No sandbagging
        working party tired.

Wiring M.L. completed, double row of knife
        rests & French wire.
        Second row of knife rests from M
        round N bombing Post.
        Second row of knife rests from P round
        S bombing Post.
        Second row of knife rests in front of
        S.20.

        50 knife rests altogether were placed,
        all that were available.
        A complaint was made that wire was
        thin round South Bombing Post.
        Everywhere it was double thickness well

possible knife rests used.

Night 19/20. __Bombing Post B.__ Started sapping round but Capt Milward R.B. stopped it. Sent Ox & Bucks working party away & put his own men on. There was not room for such a number of men.

__Bombing Post A.__ Cut all trees & roots in trench up to A.
Started sapping on, made about 5 ft when Capt Milward stopped it & acted as above.
Enlarged bombing Post.

Cut small communication trench. F.E.

__Wiring.__ Stores for Trench were taken up to head of SUNKEN ROAD.
R.E. officer reconnoitred further edge of crater with Capt Milward, from B to K.

Decided that no room for trench extension, unless trench is inside the edge of crater, it would become included in the German wire round their crater.

Also no room for wire.

Also no wire placed from A to K as there is nothing to protect.
The crater itself forms a perfect obstacle

S.20 2 Reliefs, Sandbagging, parapet & doing traverses. Trench ahead of rest

Most of trench is now tenable.

Note. Sandbagging cannot be done on the top of the trenches round the craters. Earth is too loose. It must be done from the bottom of the trench up.

The position is now very <u>strong</u> from a defense point of view.
The Germans can do nothing except to crawl about between H & K a distance of about 30 yards they cannot appear over the crest owing to the loopholes at F.

The only suggestion I can offer for improvement is to extend the bombing post at A round the crater a little. Say another 15 yards & when this is done tip a few knife rests over the edge.

A few more loopholes might be added in A.F.G.

I am strongly against any trench from beyond north bombing post having been put out 115 yards round to South one. It merely gives the Germans a point in which to effect a lodgement & work up towards our lines.

Whereas now the situation is that we have a new line which is absolutely obstructed in front & good cover from view by the Germans behind our crater.

20.10.15.

Capt R.E.
O.C. 62nd Coy. R.E.

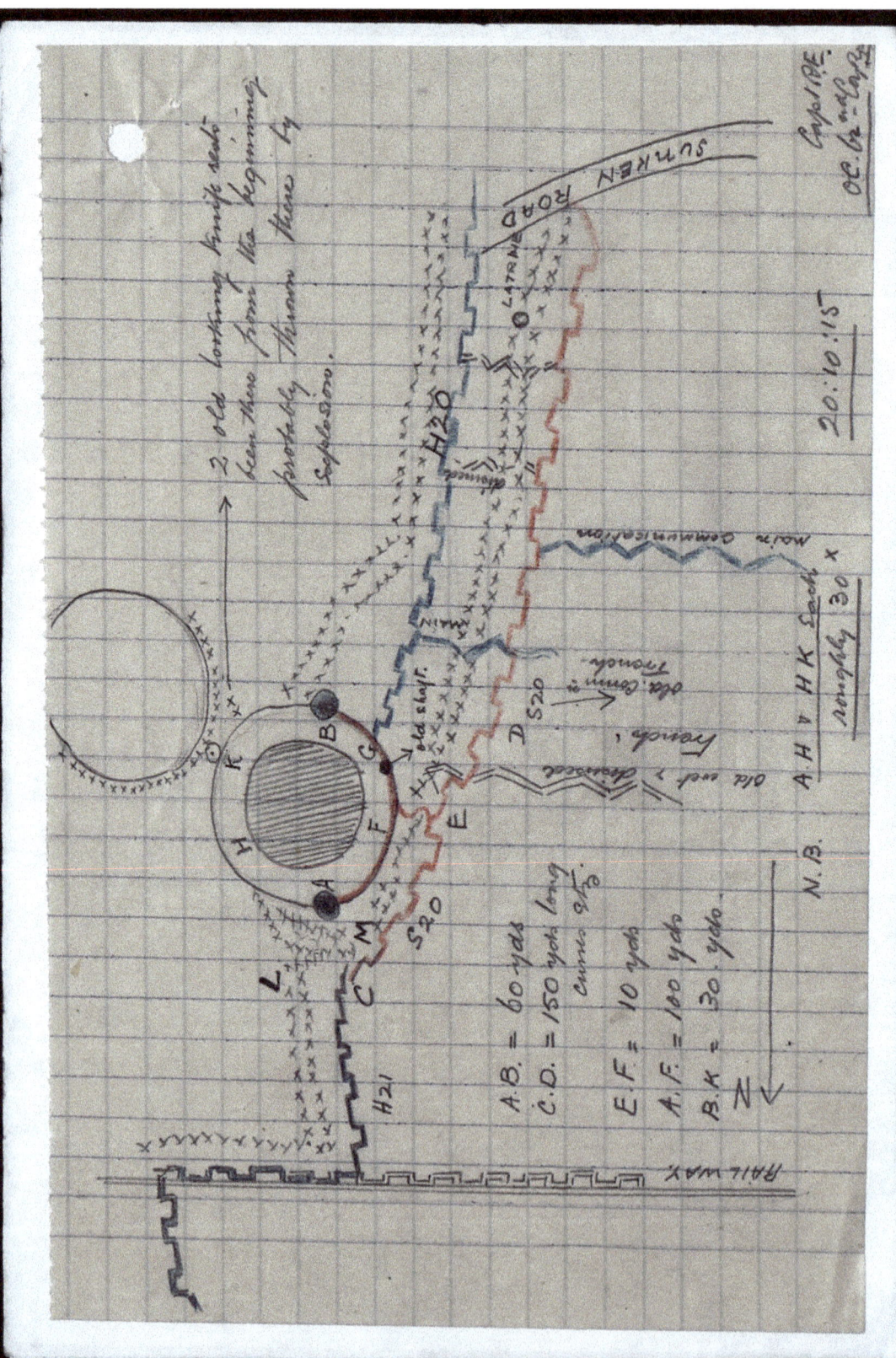

62nd F.C.R.E.
Vol: 3

14th Burma

Nov 15
& Dec

WAR DIARY
or
INTELLIGENCE SUMMARY.

Army Form C. 2118.

Place	Date	Hour	Summary of Events and Information	Remarks and references to Appendices
H.J.A.6.6	1/11/15 to 4/11/15	8 a.m.	No. 2 Section Hutting in Rest area. No. 1 & 3 tu Section improving camp for winter, paths, bivouacs erection of two new huts. Truckloads, supports on fm Lone Temple. Pontoon hills etc.	
	5/11/15	8 a.m.	No. 2 Section Hutting in Rest area. No. 1 Section told off to hutting. No. 3 to foreward work.	
	up to 18/11/15		Same programme — Division rating ½ section of No. 2 returned to join Coy. prior to going into front line. Officers reconnoitred trenches 17th & 18th.	
	19/11/15	8 a.m.	No. 1 & 3 Sections commenced 6 lines of drainage & renovating of front line trenches in two places. No. 4 & ½ No. 2 preparing materials in camp & on showground	
	20/11/15 to 25/11/15		As above. Water reduced considerably in trenches & bed of BELLEWAARDE BEEK lowered by destroying entrance to & said from POTIJZE LAKE at the BEEK. 3 M.G. emplacements taken in hand 2 at PSJ & one new near HAYMARKET. Trench about 50" Front line in relief of No. 3 Section. (in front of ↑x lung)	
	26/11/15	8 a.m.	No. 4 Section brought up as before	
	27/11/15	8 a.m.	No. 2 Section (½ section) brought up to relieve No. 1 Section, who as before.	
	28/11/15	8 a.m.	As before. II Division relieving portion allocated for @ POTIJZE before renovation by day to — by night @ Improvement of firm in front of @ x lime @ Line trenches renovation by day @ trenches by night. Division holding portion. Strength No. 1 Section brought back to supervise. About 400 in all.	

WAR DIARY
INTELLIGENCE SUMMARY.
(Erase heading not required.)

Army Form C. 2118.

Place	Date	Hour	Summary of Events and Information	Remarks and references to Appendices
H7A6B	29/11/15	8 a.m.	Work as before. No. 3 Section in Camp. R.E. in drainage parties now relieved & men available. Reinstated further working parties of II Division on wiring woods E. of POTIJZE & improving line in front of X Trenches N. of POTIJZE road. Form 20/11/15 up to this date dug out shelter made of French trophies type for 28th & Battalion Headquarters at POTIJZE chateau also shelter dugouts in CAMP track, latter assisted by 20 Belgians.	
	30/11/15	8 a.m.	Work as before. A 4 R. M.G. emplacement begun behind house near HAYMARKET. Trench about 50 yards in front of X lines built in PS₂ in frack of three portions of Trench. Nature of M.G. emplacements are in PS₂ built in front of apt. Trough/way covered by steel joists checked afit. One built of 18" brick walls in cellar depression of ruined house. Covered with steel joists & heaped bricks over all. New HAYMARKET are new PS₂ made by cutting out top portion of an even raising walls & covering with steel joists, broken brick. Gun & fire through natural openings in roof. Nothing visible from outside. One new HAYMARKET new wall built behind old wall, which was thickened & strengthened & heaped with brick, covered R.S. posts.	

WAR DIARY or INTELLIGENCE SUMMARY

Army Form C. 2118.

Place	Date	Hour	Summary of Events and Information	Remarks and references to Appendices
H7A b 6	1/12/15	6 a.m.	"Both as before".	
	2/12/15 to 8/12/15	8 a.m.	do — No. 3 section relieved No. 1.	
	9/12/15	8 a.m.	Both as before. No. 1 Section relieved No. 4 on 8/12/15. All front line dry except right of A4 + Drainage work completed. Drains nothing any mt. Then C3 thick glaud made drainage very difficult. New culvert made 2' lower part of A3 where BEEK cut through POTIJZE road, dam at bottom of LAKE E cut away at foot where BEEK cut through POTIJZE + ST JEAN to allow flood water BEEK left away. Road cut through between POTIJZE + ST JEAN to allow flood water BEEK to drain. All water mud LANCER FARM locked 18" to small X trenches HAYMARKET to drain properly. X line renovated in two pieces POTIJZE ROAD to HAYMARKET + for 75Y north of X line renovated. A new line of pine placed between the two old lines in front of X trenches from PICCADILLY. A new line of pine POTIJZE road to right of pine. POTIJZE road to STRAND renovated + line of pine made between two X line N.O. POTIJZE road to left of section held. All existing lines from POTIJZE ROAD to left of section held. Woods N.E. of POTIJZE ch.feon thoroughly mud up + trenchwork at VINERY renovated. POTIJZE defences S. of road renovated + drained. Portion N. of road rather heavily shelled + not completed. 4 M.G. Emplacements to above described completed. A.G. emplacement in POTIJZE WOOD to fire down VERLOREN HOEK road. Plan of drainage of sector attached. Dugouts for 2 scts of Battalion Headquarters at POTIJZE Dugouts for Keeve Battalion of CANAL BANK.	Casualties Pt. Banks wounded 2/12/15 Shll. 1 OR died of wounds 3/12/15 Gsh. L.Ch. 1 NCO wounded Shll. 9/12/15 Shll. Pt. Banks died wounds 12/12/15 Shll. T.C.F.
	16/12/15	6 a.m.	Section 5 relieved in withdrawal of Divn from front line.	

WAR DIARY
or
INTELLIGENCE SUMMARY.
(Erase heading not required.)

Army Form C. 2118.

Instructions regarding War Diaries and Intelligence Summaries are contained in F. S. Regs., Part II. and the Staff Manual respectively. Title pages will be prepared in manuscript.

Place	Date	Hour	Summary of Events and Information	Remarks and references to Appendices
17 B.6.6	17/10/15 to 28/10/15		Company resting with Divisional rest. Halting by one section provided. Arrangements made to find in all winter equipment its made arrangements for a move.	
	29/10/15	8 a.m.	Co. visited new trenches by night. Front line in a dreadful state. No wiring - dine only held by a series of outposts disconnected from each other. To visit which circular journey of 5 to 6 miles made thus. Defences of CANAL BANK in which F31 disorganised condition, no proper accommodation for troops etc.	

Trenches mostly falling to pieces & having very difficult side their bins. Only way to make F34, F33, F32, F31 would be to put in U frames with good revetment & drain down the trenches themselves.

→ strut put in with head own keeping board heads
9"×3"   9"   3"×3"
3/6"

Army Form C. 2118.

WAR DIARY
or
INTELLIGENCE SUMMARY.
(Erase heading not required.)

Place	Date	Hour	Summary of Events and Information	Remarks and references to Appendices
H7 B. 6.6	30/9/15	8 a.m.	CO. visited trenches by day. Chine, FARGATE etc.	See plan
	30/9/15	8 a.m.	½ section No 2 sent up to lay duckboards in CANAL BANK for work superintended on bridges.	
	1/10/15	8 a.m.	Commenced work on relaying F.33 by working up from stream. Very difficult job as route & road seems unusually good portion of WYATT'S LANE where parallel to old fallen in pit across S.33 & F.33. From head of WYATT'S LANE to F.33 too open & dangerous in full view of enemy.	1 Sapper wounded.
		2 p.m.	Told officer to superintend work on dugouts in CANAL BANK. I have to superintend making of Knife rests at HODGER FARM.	
			Officers and men detailed to superintend work on C. line.	See plan
			Co. made reconnaissance to see if better way could be found to work portion of F.33. Found route by leaving FARGATE just No of Bridge 72 & working up stream to junction of F.34 & F.33. No 3 Section not available - taken for butting.	
2/10/15 to 10/10/15		8 a.m.	Same work as above. ½ section No. 2 on bridges & superintending work on C.line, superintending construction of dugouts in CANAL BANK, making knife rests. Relaying F.33 & F.34 their usual fortnightly No. 4 section relieved by No. 1 on night 7/8 etc. Broke on the whole poor. the Trenches in the marne. in the night travels themselves very difficult being blocked with debris of many dugouts come down. Also the Thaw itself was very difficult & in going astray enemy no casualties. Finally working parties kept on going astray & lost knowledge of places in sent. Finally working parties infantry towards the old of this period all sent out same men this new sector. in front of front line & had begun to establish to the bombing.	

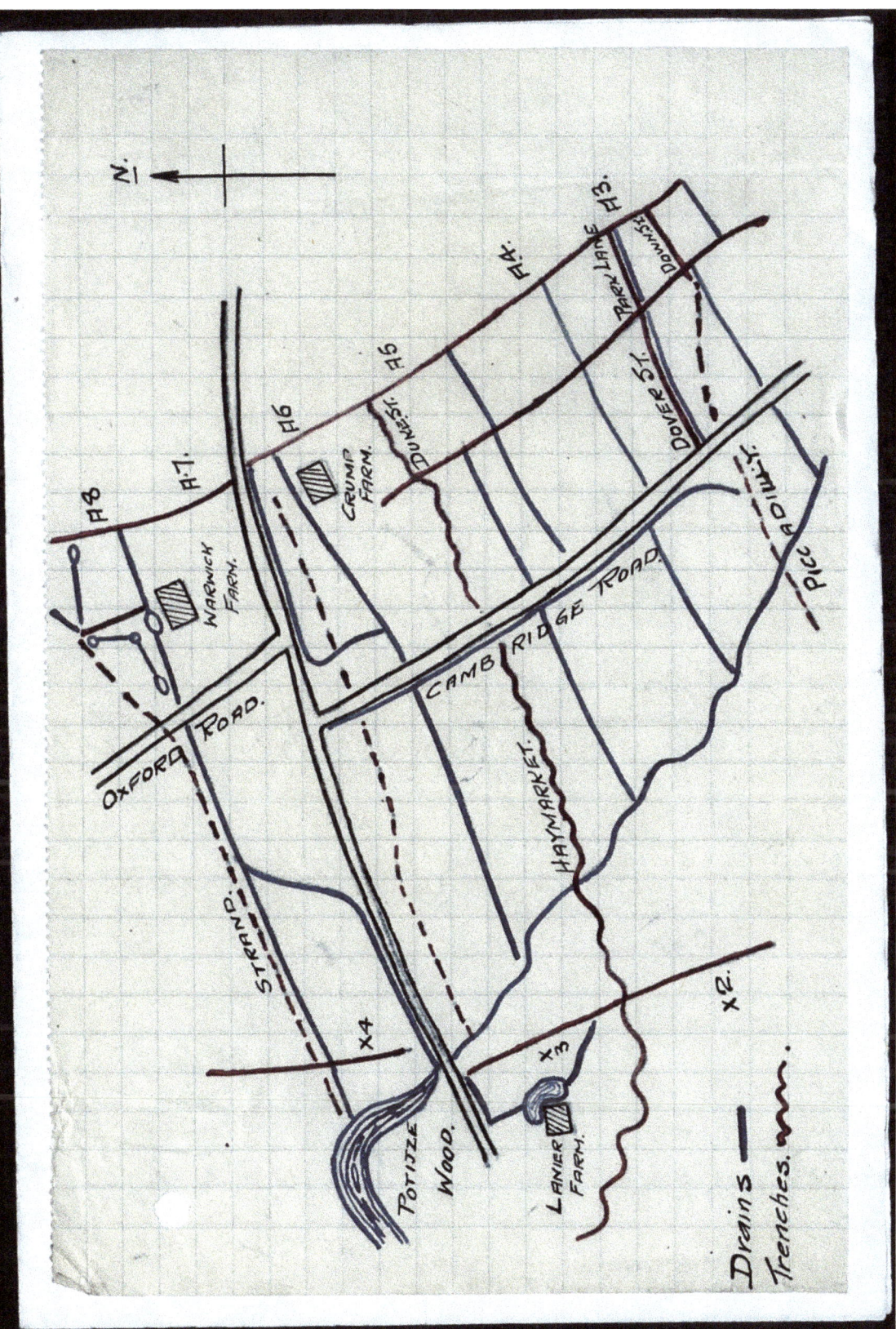

62 w 7CRE.
Vol: 5
17/12/15 – 31/1/16.

14

WAR DIARY

INTELLIGENCE SUMMARY

Army Form C. 2118.

Place	Date	Hour	Summary of Events and Information	Remarks and references to Appendices
4 7 B 6 6	10/1/16	8a.m.	2/Lieut Satterthwaite took out working party of a CO. made reconnaissance of a new file was laid from hd. of WELLGATE to S32. In consequence track heads on the filled in up WELLGATE known, thence by S32 to WELLGATE drain & made the filled in up WELLGATE known, thence by strand time to life of road. Therefore a small track will have to be dug & posts held at F31 & behind. 2 Men with 2 infantry bricklayers were put on making M.G. emplacement near BARNSLEY ROAD. Also CO. arranged for 2 tunnelled M.G. emplacements of FARGATE, both done by drill mining. Section by Carpenters to make the loopholes bases which will carry the concrete. No. 4 Section were taken off track on Cline so own yft so light it was impossible to F83. No. 2 Section relieved of all other duties so as to tunnel onto bridges 7Z, 7Y, 6E, 6D, 6x, 6C, & 6w. Sewers put up on bridges 6D & 7Z, handrail under Lefthandbridge 7Z & 7Y improved	
	11/1/16 to 2/1/16	8a.m.	8 men of No. 3 Section taken to superintend construction of dug outs & rebuild ing by him in CAMP L BANK, 4 by day & four by night, these 8 being relieved by 8 men of section on that line returning. Resting men of company employed in making new camp ready. 24 Sapts attached for work with R.E. permanently so as to been about entrenchments. Work on Cline. Butts 9 & 10 completed & connected up, communication trenches made. Butt 5 completed. Butts 9 & 10 done & begun on Butt 4, communication trench & parapet made, work in hand. Dug outs in 9 & 10 done & begun on 4. C.O. arranged for Sgt machine guns with B.M.G.O. at Nightingale Cottage & Ayer So Farm Khien enemy's communication. Other tunnel dug out to bridge enemy's presently. One tunnel dug out off FARGATE completed.

WAR DIARY
or
INTELLIGENCE SUMMARY.
(Erase heading not required.)

Army Form C. 2118.

Place	Date	Hour	Summary of Events and Information	Remarks and references to Appendices
H7 B66	22/1/16 to 3/1/16	20.m	No. 2 Section alternating. Bridges. Renewal of Bridges 6c taken in hand, let from repaired hand as bridge has now more than ½ demolished. Bridge 6D broken in, repaired. Seven renewed. Bridge 72 broken in, repaired. Spare timber for repairs collected & put in set offs dug from the approaches. The demolition slabs gone over & renewed where they had become deteriorated.	1 Sapper wounded.

C.H.R. Cheney
Capt. R.E.
O.C. 6 tray R.E.

WAR DIARY or INTELLIGENCE SUMMARY

Army Form C. 2118.

Place	Date	Hour	Summary of Events and Information	Remarks and references to Appendices
H7 B f.b	22/1/16 to 31/1/16	8 a.m.	No. 1 & No. 4 Section alternating 6 nights at work & 6 resting. **Work done.** **Cline.** Completed shelters C22 + C23 (Butts numbered by Division). Jim Putts connected together by breastwork. Extension of 22 to BARNSLEY ROAD. Six dug outs provided. Two strong ones with heavy frames & steel girder roofs. Two small + light 2 men dug outs. One light 4 men dug out. Parapet thickened up throughout. Length opened about 70 yards. **Butt (8.** The old portion of breastwork completely renovated together, MG emplacement rebuilt. Communication trench built & protected by hurdle revetment. 5 dug outs provided. Two very strong with heavy frames + rail or girder roof. 2, 2 men dug outs of light pattern + one 4 man dug out of light pattern. Length of trench about 70 yards. **Butt 17.** Begun. Extension of two firebays on each wing repaired, also 5 dug outs. 2 dug outs. One strong one light made + extensive hyum work nearly completed. Of getting up stores. **ZWAAN HOF Brick replacement.** Completed – a little thickening of roof required. F.39. A large portion retained with U frames, suspended noted & trench boards. Some new work has been noted. Most of the work was towards the western end so as to connect up practically with F.35, though a small extension was also carried out towards the eastern end.	

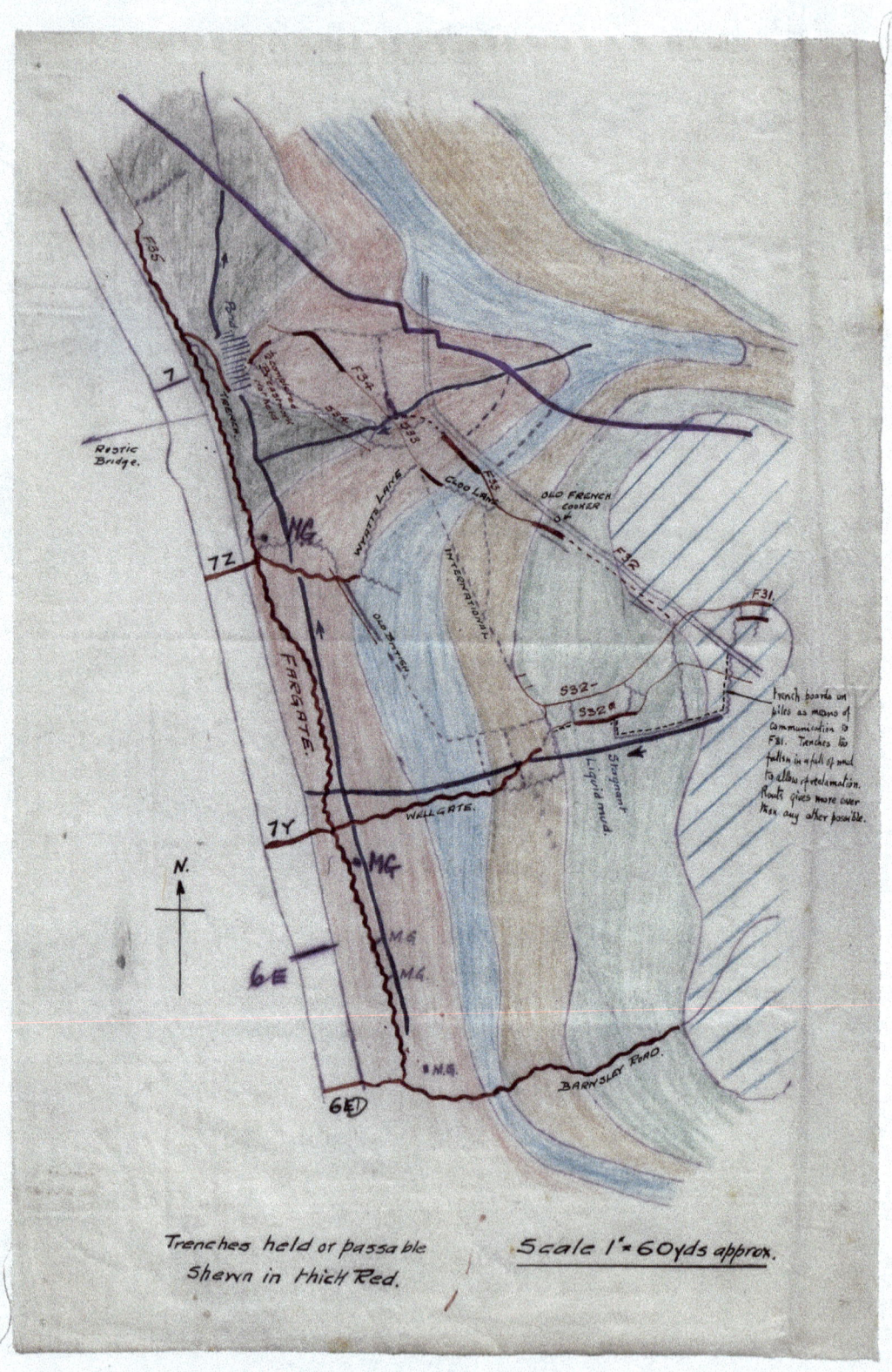

Trenches held or passable Shewn in thick Red.

Scale 1"= 60 yds approx.

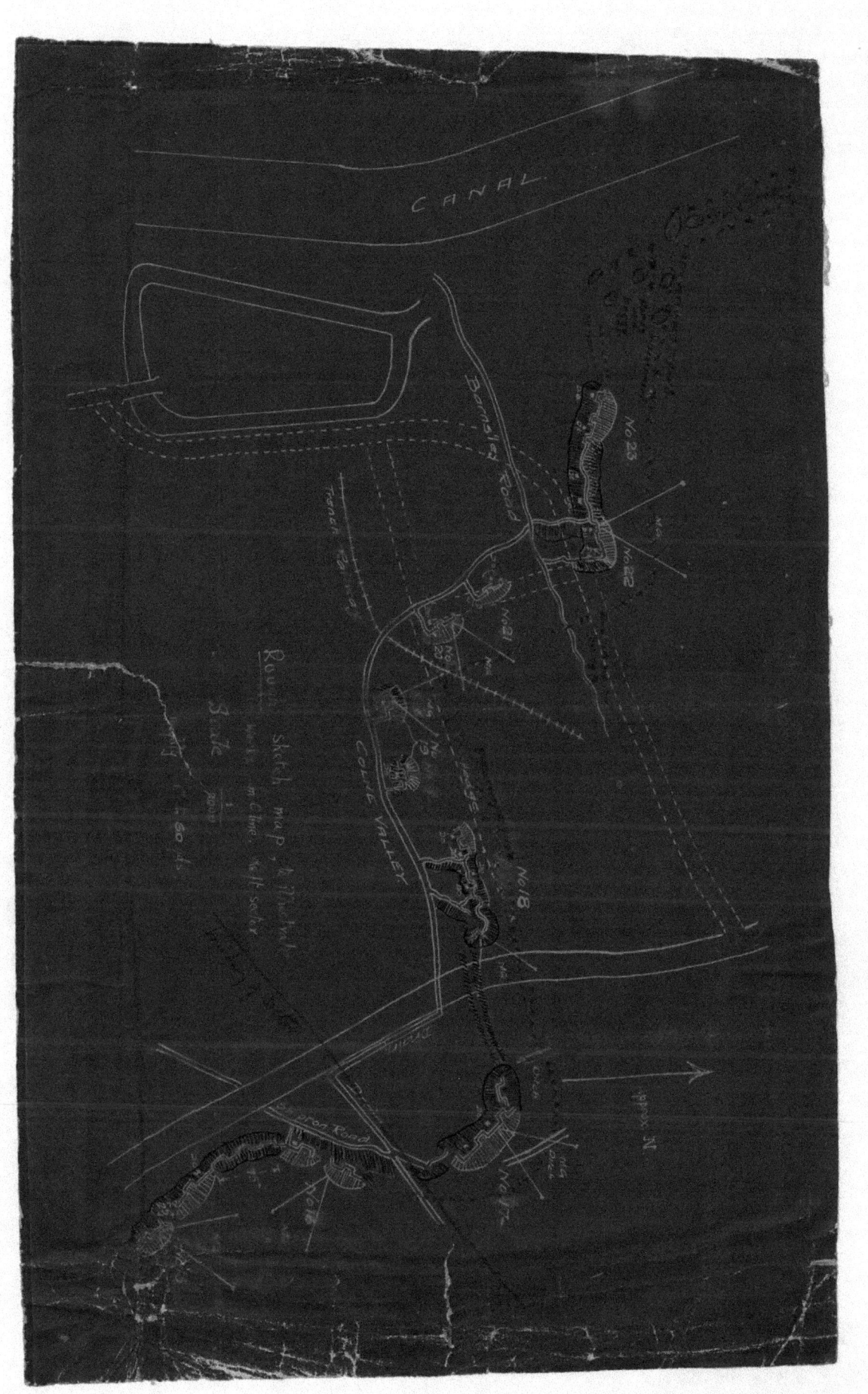

6220
J. C. R. E.
14ᵗʰ Dec
Vol. 6

Army Form C. 2118.

WAR DIARY
or
INTELLIGENCE SUMMARY.
(Erase heading not required.)

Place	Date	Hour	Summary of Events and Information	Remarks and references to Appendices
Hy B.C.L.	11/2/16 to 11/3/16	8 a.m.	Nos 1 & 4 Sections alternating. work done. Cline. Butts 21 + 23 Bridge traverse in connecting trench made. Block in loopholes over balls in place. BARNSLEY ROAD begun, with loopholes over balls in place. Butt 18. Completed. Butt 17. Proceeding. Parados + dugouts still wanting. 2 new M.G. emplacements constructed of FARGATE, one north of WYATT'S LANE one south of WELLGATE. Covered communication trench to each emplacement made about 6'x 6' - heavy frames - two rows of steel girders opposite ways set in cement. loophole with girders and concrete above.	RE 1 Sapt. wounded
			No. 2 Section. ½ section alternating. Bridges. Bridge 6c. completed. Bridge 6W. broken & repaired. Bridge 72. screen again repaired. Collection of repair materials & stacking of same proceeding.	
11/2/16	8 a.m.		Completion of above work by Nos 1 & 4 sections on night 9/10 Th. No. 3 section returned to unit from huttings on afternoon 10th. No. 2 section relieved from bridge work on night 11/12 Th. by 2/st Div R.E.	
12/2/16	8 a.m.			

C.H. Chomneys Capt.
O.C. 62 Cy R.E.

Army Form C. 2118.

WAR DIARY
or
INTELLIGENCE SUMMARY.
(Erase heading not required.)

Instructions regarding War Diaries and Intelligence Summaries are contained in F. S. Regs., Part II and the Staff Manual respectively. Title pages will be prepared in manuscript.

Place	Date	Hour	Summary of Events and Information	Remarks and references to Appendices
HERZEELE	14/2/16	8 a.m.	Whole Coy. marched to HERZEELE via POPERINGHE, WATOU. Dull grey cold morn.	
	15/2/16	—	Coy. resting at HERZEELE in billets.	
	20/2/16	8 a.m.	Marched to ESQUELBEC arriving at station 3.30 p.m. Entrained reaching LONGUE MAU (AMIENS goods station) at 3.30 a.m. March to new billets.	
	22/2/16	8 a.m.	Reached new billets at VILLERS BOCAGE 9 m. N. of AMIENS at 11 a.m. 22/2/16	
	24/2/16	8 a.m.	Rested at VILLERS BOCAGE in billets	
	25/2/16	8 a.m.	Marched at 10 a.m. arriving GEZAINCOURT 3 p.m. Heavy snow.	
	26/2/16	6 a.m.	near DOULLENS. Marched at 10 a.m. arriving LUCHEUX at 8.30 p.m. billeted for night as impossible to find further billets ordered at SUS ST LEGER. Very difficult marching, very trying, state of roads. Reg't shd. all horses at VILLERS BOCAGE, again at GEZAINCOURT, horsed horses were after this village on country that run out of quails.	
	27/2/16	8 a.m.	Marched at 10 a.m. arriving SUS ST LEGER 12 noon.	
	28/2/16	8 a.m.	Rested in billets SUS ST LEGER.	
	29/2/16	8 a.m.	on 29/2/16 Marched at 9.15 a.m. arriving BARLY 3 p.m.	

C.R. Cheney, Captain,
O.C. ...

Army Form C. 2118.

WAR DIARY
of 62nd Fld Coy R.E. 10th Div.

INTELLIGENCE SUMMARY.

Instructions regarding War Diaries and Intelligence Summaries are contained in F. S. Regs., Part II. and the Staff Manual respectively. Title pages will be prepared in manuscript.

(Erase heading not required.)

Place	Date	Hour	Summary of Events and Information	Remarks and references to Appendices
	1/3/16	8 a.m.	Arrived previous day BARLY. 3 p.m.	
	2/3/16	8 a.m.	Marched at 2 p.m. arrived DAINVILLE 6.30 p.m. Billets.	
	3/3/16		Billetted in DAINVILLE. Stables arranged for horses as they had previously been left in the open behind railway embankment. Improved accommodation for men. Printed latrine & washing accommodation.	
	4/3/16	8 a.m.	Commenced erection of baths for Coy.	
	5/3/16		HQ Brigade took over trenches night 5/6 F. Nos 2 & 3 Sections marched up to billets in ARRAS night 5/6 F.	
	6/3/16		Co. went round diff. half of trenches. Nos 2 & 3 Section arranging billets in ARRAS making suitable for accommodation. No. 4 Section at billets in DAINVILLE.	
	7/5/16	8 a.m.	Co. went round Right half of trenches. No. 2 Section commenced work on Bde. Hdqs. Battle dugout. BOISVILLE. One dugout pivoted made by trench entrance was holed also & dummy roof of c. iron was completion & roof strengthening.	
	8/3/16	8 a.m.	Was Mill in front of ACHICOURT. Roof strengthening where necessary. In my opinion the might was a great deal (about 7') for the lowest row of piles bearing over the span. So much so that strict from a shell may have broken them. There was an absence of any strutting to prevent the side frames collapsing or inclining towards each other. The chalk walls were good hard still this was a defect. The final section was made thicker (see on ...)	Sketch ⊗

[Sketch showing cross-section with dimensions: 7', about 10', top of piles 6"×6" sawbuck, 9"×9" hammer piles, still forming piles, left still 4' breadth pieces]

Capt R. Cheney
Capt.

WAR DIARY of 62nd Field Coy R.E. 14th Div
INTELLIGENCE SUMMARY

Place: DAINVILLE
Date: 12/3/16
Hour: 8 a.m.

Air space with vertical ends

about 3'6"

→ barbed ¾" wire well fastened
→ ¾" bar etc
→ ¾" flat steel bars 8¾" with fed together with ¾" wire arranged with army wire netting possibly fixed in neighbourhood. Over all a 1" iron bars 6'x ... placed vertically — has ... the about bars

Section of roof

→ ½" wire intertwoven thickly

→ heavy nails alternately laid & well tied in with ¼" wire

All roads, wire & ¾" round bars were ready on site which enabled work to be completed as quickly.

No 4 Section employed on latrines, washing accommodation, recreation room, & huts for troops in DAINVILLE.

No 1 Section improving existing mined dugouts in DAINVILLE.

Portion of No 4 Section detailed to improve dugouts in right sector. Work entailed made up of 2 shelters 20 feet long with 6 foot thick traverse in middle to be completed as per sketch (X) about 8ft without steel toofing. Side frames strutting now required & lateral struts between frames & front sides inclining inwards retaining ...

Two mined dugouts about 25' deep, 20' long at bottom & 2 entrances & do complete
One mined dugout of these dimensions & two entrances strutted.
Two mined dugouts of these dimensions strutted & connections between entrances made.

(Y) 400 feet long, 5 dugouts

(signatures)

Army Form C. 2118.

WAR DIARY
of 2nd Fd Coy R.E. 14th Div.

INTELLIGENCE SUMMARY.

(Erase heading not required.)

Instructions regarding War Diaries and Intelligence Summaries are contained in F.S. Regs., Part II. and the Staff Manual respectively. Title pages will be prepared in manuscript.

Place	Date	Hour	Summary of Events and Information	Remarks and references to Appendices
DAINVILLE	17/3/16	8a.m.	Remainder Section as above.	
	18/3/16	8a.m.	No. 2 Section. Completed headquarters dugouts as indicated above, returned to DAINVILLE.	One Sapper wounded working in dugouts in Right Section
			No. 4 Section. completed baths etc, moved up to ARRAS revealed on Sole Section on above mentioned dugouts. Have found very efficient & comfortable. Sketch of baths as made attached.	
			No. 3 Section. M.G. emplacement as above.	
			No. 1 Section. moved to BERNEVILLE to work under Adjutant R.E. on hutting accommodation at BERNEVILLE – SIMENCOURT.	
	19/3/16	8a.m.	No. 2 Section. making another set of hutting arrangements – 3 miles in truck – holes bolts taken & used in huts. Making bricks, cement floor took under spray of bathing accommodation. Remainder as above.	
	20/3/16	8a.m.	No. 3 Section. on completion of M.G. emplacement returned to DAINVILLE, No. 2 Section.	
			No. 2 Section. commenced new M.G. emplacement at CHATEAU RONVILLE, semi turn-concrete, (Sketches to follow in next month's Diary).	
			No. 3 Section. continued with dugouts in DAINVILLE. ½ Section had to return 2 nights to M.G. emplacement they made to reduce width of door by 2'8" by filling concrete layers & walls of door each side. This made the thickness of side & rifle loopholes greater.	
			Remainder same.	
			No. 6 Section. Completed dugouts marked (Y) above. Commenced Dressing station & work in Railway Embankment ACHICOURT. (Sketches to follow in next month's Diary)	

C.R. [signature] Capt.

WAR DIARY

of 62nd F.W. Co. R.E. 14th Div.

INTELLIGENCE SUMMARY.

(Erase heading not required.)

Army Form C. 2118.

Place	Date	Hour	Summary of Events and Information	Remarks and references to Appendices
	28/3/16	8a.m.	**No 3 Section.** Commenced 4 emplacements for 4.5" Howitzers at DAINVILLE. [sketches of ground plan and section A.B. with dimensions and notes including "9'x3' silo", "4 wooden steps from 1' to 6cm", "5' high inside", "6' inside", "10'6"", "bayonets", "B. shelling", "one shell hit", "flat roof 3¼" thick", "6" concrete layer with cement extended on that layer", "Section A.B."]	
	31/3/16	8a.m.	**No 4 Section.** Completed dug out (T) above and (Z) with a translator with cement about a sill with ashes proceeding with bayonets (S) & drawing station. Remainder continuing with works demanded. **General** Sector quiet having whole time practically. Trenches in this sector manned by R.E. have been given some nice instructional work to do. Damman tripod large scale map by help of aeroplane photographs of whole front. Our officers made detailed reports of trench system at RONVILLE & ACHICOURT villages.	Capt Chaney Capt R.E. 1/4/16

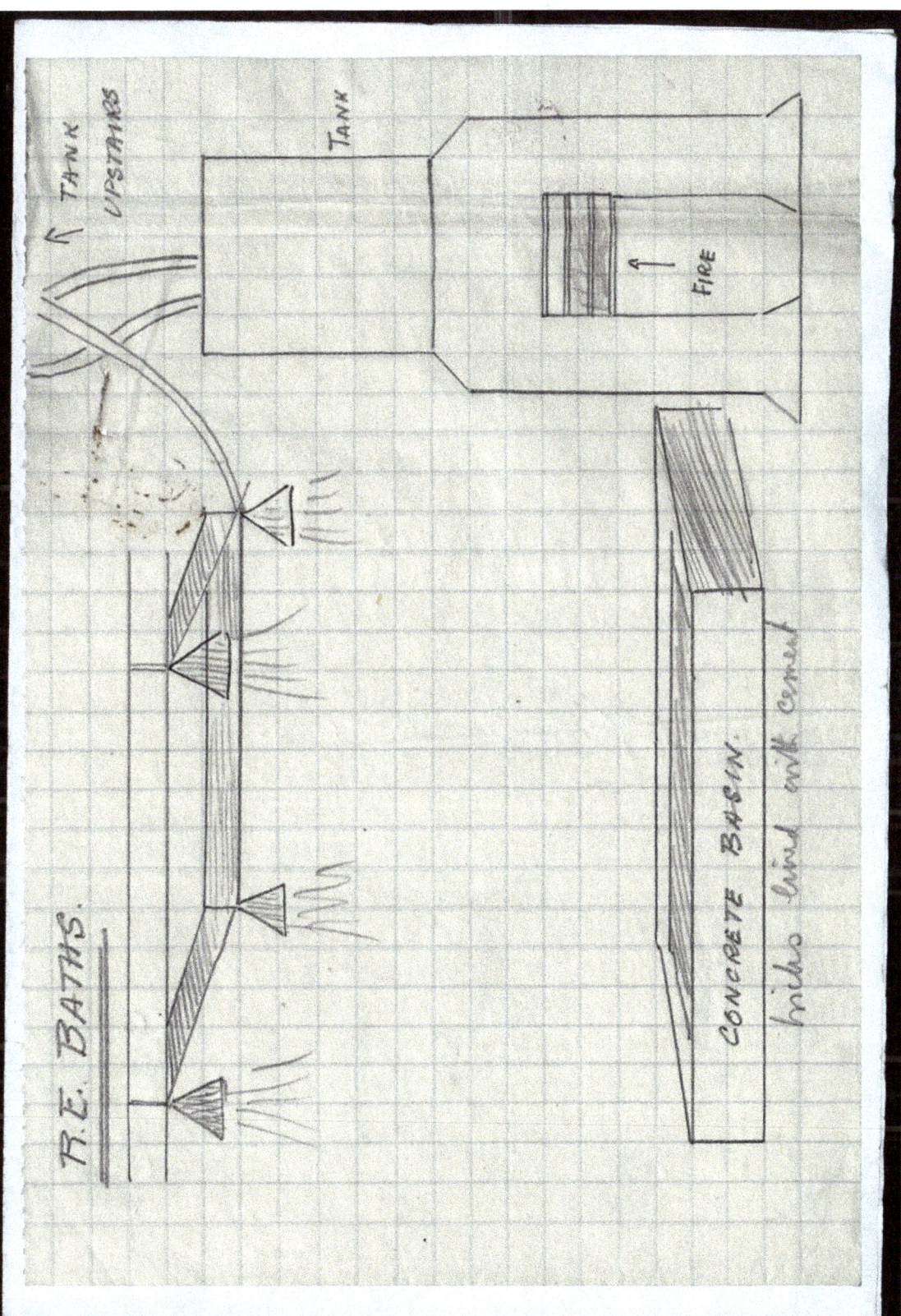

62 F.E RE of below. RE
Vol 8

Army Form C. 2118.

WAR DIARY
or
INTELLIGENCE SUMMARY.
(Erase heading not required.)

XIV

Place	Date	Hour	Summary of Events and Information	Remarks and references to Appendices
DAINVILLE	1/4/16 to 14/4/16	8 a.m.	No. 1 Section & No. 2 Section still detached from under CRE at BERNEVILLE. Matting water supply etc. at work on Farm-annexe M.G. emplacement at CHATEAU, DAINVILLE. Drawings of completed structure as attached. Also commenced recomplete splinter proof M.G. emplacement in the line on entrance trench. Commenced small mined dugout for same with two entrances off trench. No. 2 Section completed 3 emplacements for 4.5" Howitzers (sketches given in last month's Diary) the 4th emplacement was some completed by the R.A. undertaking to finish it. No. 4 Section proceeding with dugouts (S) above. One completed & a fresh begun in Blue. This dugout had 4 entrances mined to 20 ft depth. No entrance commenced. This dugout & 2 officers' stabling & supervised chalk in mine, workers training. Signal stabling length 70'. Section B(V)(V). Also another mined in dugout and wanted length — which two entrances were made that wanted day not taken in hand (W-) connecting together. Bearing Station completed with exception of some finishing touches & ventilating. White was painted inside with white enamel dried with linseed oil, on installation. Sketches attached. Pushed with further provisions to get rid of the water with one dugout S as above also with V & W.	
	15/4/16	8 a.m.	No. 2 Section moved up to ARRAS & proceeded No. 4 Section moved up to DAINVILLE. General making double huts to put in billets at DAINVILLE so as to increase accommodation. 3 men told off to repair pumps & wells in RUE DE GEN. JOFFRE at ACHICOURT which were either damaged or out of order. No. 2 & 4 Sections as above.	CRE Cheney Capt OC 62 FE RE

1577 Wt. W10791/1773 500,000 1/15 D. D. & L. A.D.S.S./Forms/C. 2118.

Army Form C. 2118.

762 Coy R.E.

WAR DIARY
or
INTELLIGENCE SUMMARY.
(Erase heading not required.)

Place	Date	Hour	Summary of Events and Information	Remarks and references to Appendices
RANVILLE	17/4/16	8 a.m.	No. 2 Section. Men working on LILLE Road dugout near M.G. emplacement on the left. Shelled 4 times at intervals of ½ an hour. Men went indoors. Few annoying shrapnels in the field which were rather shallow. 2 R.E. wounded. So work was stopped for the day. Walls of strengthening cellar in small house fronting from RONVILLE to LEGROUPE DES MAISONS completed. A spare room was built about 12' × 12' × 7' high — space between that and the roof of cellar was filled up with rubble. Gun about 2' to 3' below thickness. Was the wall to be a layer of T.O.P. which was situated in the little house above. There was heavy fire with rifle about 2' thick. Remainder same as before. Site for M.G. emplacement near junction of HARDY STREET railway unmoirised with O.C. Machine Gun Company. Decided by G.O.C. that this should be only splinter proof as it is on a site invisible to enemy & Bretisim left shall be left for a week to see it also, that work on small wind dugout and, so that enemy shall turn this attention to something else.	1 O.R. wounded 1 Supp.
	18/4/16	8 a.m.	O.C. Coy, O.C. No. 2 Section & O.C. Machine Gun Coy, remomissed position for new M.G. emplacement near GROUPE DES MAISONS.	
	19/4/16	8 a.m.	No. 2 Section commenced work on that two machine gun emplacements. Remainder as above.	
	22/4/16	8 a.m.	No. 3 Section finished remaining dugout (S) above. Continued with 4 entrance dugout (V) but ceased work on dugout (W) as B.G.C. did not consider it worth while to go on with this dugout	

Army Form C. 2118.

WAR DIARY
of 62nd Fld Co R.E. 14th Div

INTELLIGENCE SUMMARY.

(Erase heading not required.)

Instructions regarding War Diaries and Intelligence Summaries are contained in F. S. Regs., Part II. and the Staff Manual respectively. Title pages will be prepared in manuscript.

Place	Date	Hour	Summary of Events and Information	Remarks and references to Appendices
DAINVILLE			Length of dugout about 35 feet. Besides this work No 2 Section forwarded with section of a stood dugout to which the excavation had been partly done & some drains about 20 foot long. *[Sketch: roof of dugout with steel sheeting, 6"x6" posts, 4"x4" struts between rafters, air space, etc. — annotations: "9in of 6" posts binding round", "steel sheeting", "8in transoms across roof", "about 9'", "Steel rods 18" apart", "4"x4" struts between rafters about 10", "Iron frames not to start inches about 10'", "7'"]* No. 3 Section forwarded with ferro concrete M.G. Emplacement examined by French at RONVILLE *[Sketch plan of MG emplacement with dimensions 17', 10', 3'6", 4", 4'3" — annotations: "M.G. loopholes", "A", "B"]* round iron 3/8" diameter about 1' apart held tied in with wire taken up with trough. Concrete mix:- 1. 2. 3 2. grit sand & granite chippings with trouble. French had completed walls & roof as far as door beginning from left outside of emplacement, just laying rails & covering with about 3" concrete & filling in sand. The portion from A to B had not been completed when it was hit by a big shell & destroyed. At sections A & B walls had to be cut down thoroughly & walls of this portion had to be cleared.	

G.R. Cheeney
Capt.

WAR DIARY
INTELLIGENCE SUMMARY
Army Form C. 2118.

Place	Date	Hour	Summary of Events and Information	Remarks and references to Appendices
			After reconnaissance by O.C. & O.C. No 3 Section had a tunnel M.G. Emplacement was commenced under a road at N.30 in front line. Intention being that nothing should show that the tp.g. should traffic to pass down the front-line run through a slit in the bank of the road. An old dugout excavated having a roof thickness of 10ft + about 15ft long was made use of. It was estimated that length of tunnel would eventually be about 60'.	
			No 3 Section also had in hand a dugout ½ completed the tripod as a sleeping room at Battn. H.dqr. (right).	
			No 4 Section during hours at DAINVILLE, making hands approximating with mounting for Lewis with disposing of tropical plates. Infantry Park. Improvements Guns, assisting strengthening of R.A.M.E. cellars in SO CREAK. Remainder as before.	
26/4/16	8a.m.		O.C. delivered lecture on R.E. work to Senior C.A. Officers course at ST POL.	
			No 3 section making splinterproof latrines in garden of Brigade Hdqrs in ARRAS. Also splinterproof latrines for Bde. Hdqr. dugouts near mill near ACHICOURT.	
29/4/16	8a.m.		Territorial ½ section assisting in front line work (Cont) by S.of E. Durand. Finished lorry which emplacement in house at RONVILLE. Commenced time-concrete emplacement in house in ACHICOURT.	
30/4/16	8a.m.		Remainder as before. No was made 520 active heads for tunnels during 2 months it has been in the line.	

A.R. Roomy
Capt
OC 6/62/17

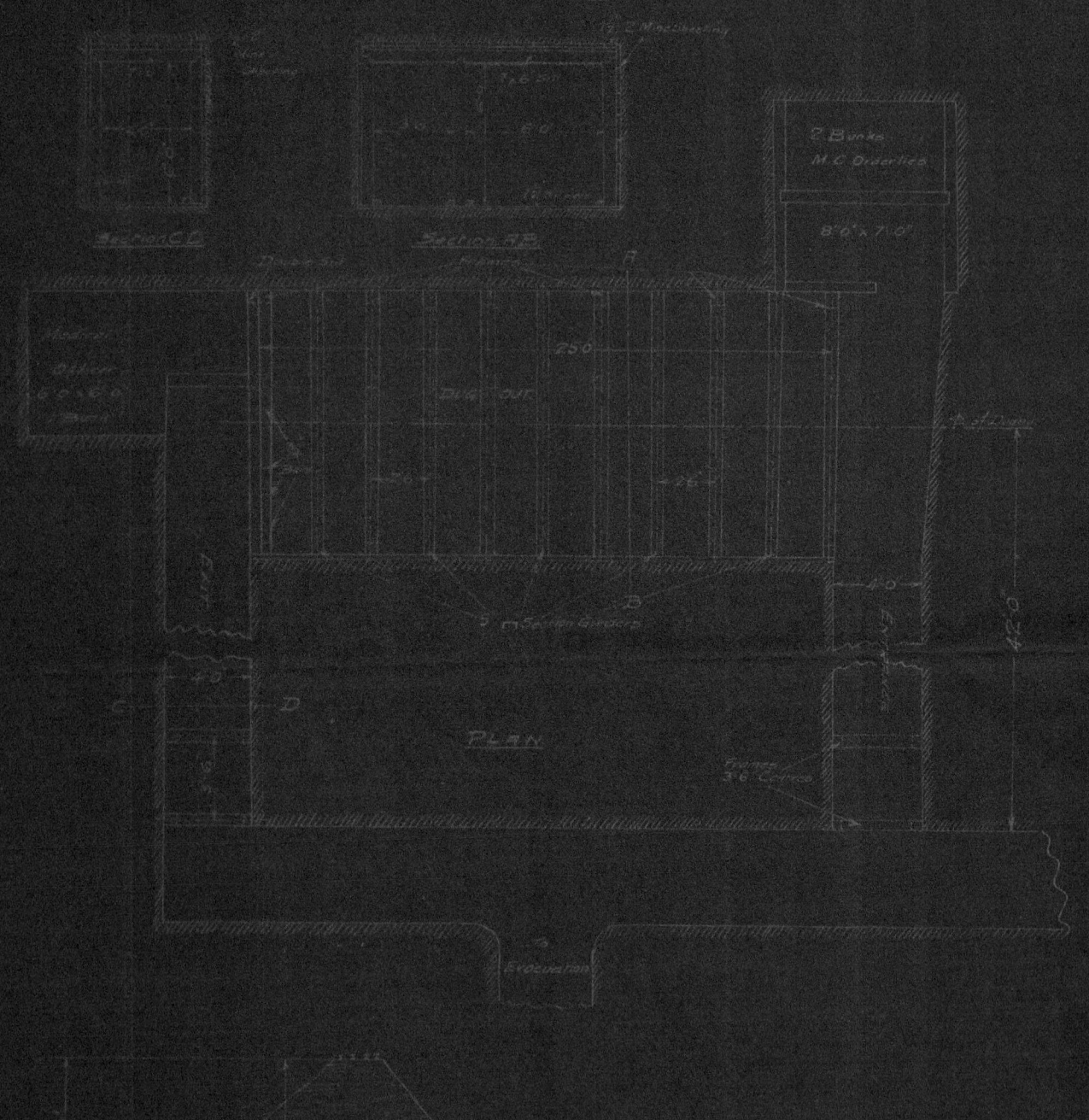

M.G. Emplacement
Chateau Ronville

Cross Section

Longitudinal Section

Plan

Small scale plan and Section shewing position of Dugout under Emplacement

Plan

Section

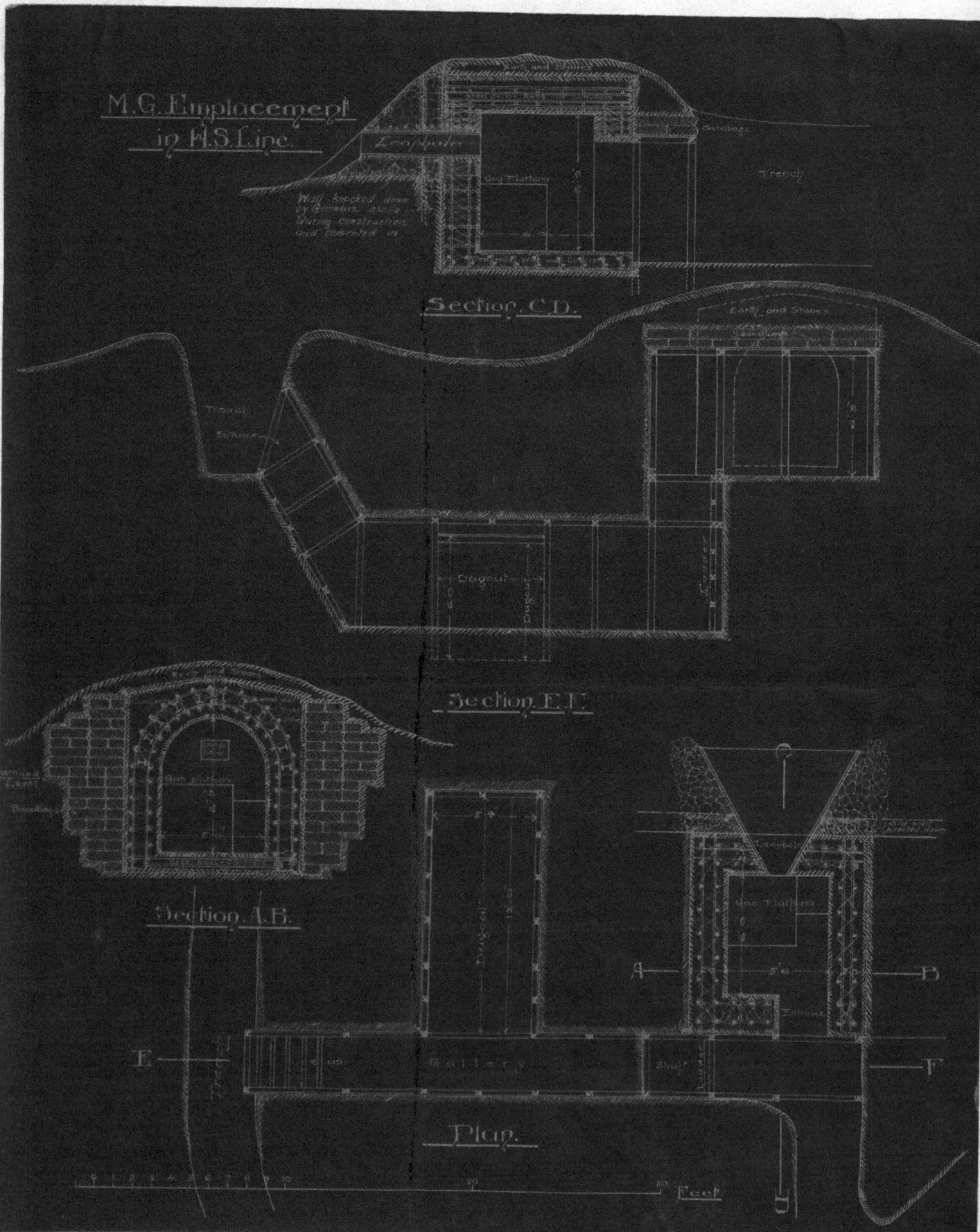

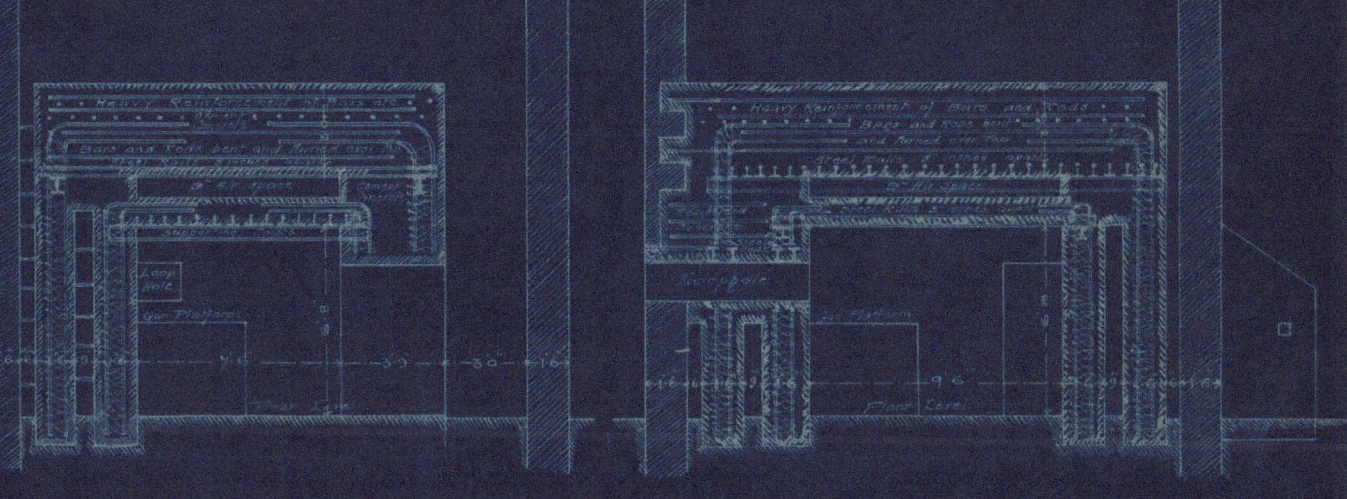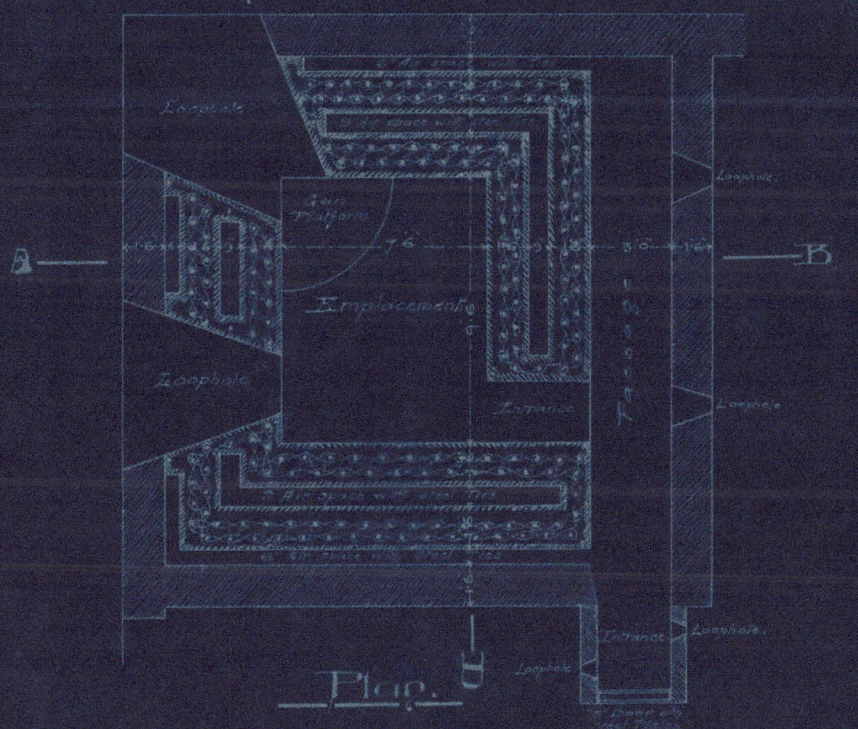

Army Form C. 2118.

XIV
of 62bg RE
VOL 9

WAR DIARY
or
INTELLIGENCE SUMMARY.
(Erase heading not required.)

Place	Date	Hour	Summary of Events and Information	Remarks and references to Appendices
DAINVILLE	1/5/16	8 a.m.	Distribution of 60:—	
			No 2 Section — Machine Gun Emplacement splinterproof near Railway in ash dumping ground. Machine Gun Emplacement semi-bombproof in Cline near GROUPE DES MAISONS. Splinterproof latrine in Bde Adjs Mess. " " to Advanced position near Hill.	
			No 3 Section — Machine-gun Emplacement from Advanced tunnel in front of frontline H.30. Officers' sleeping room dugout Right Batt⁰. 4 entrance dug out 6'×50'.	
			No 4 Section — DAINVILLE, finishing odd jobs.	
			No 1 Section — BERNEVILLE under C.R.E. sinking watersupply.	
			Forw ½ section — Advanced Emplacements M.G. Emplacement.	
	7/5/16	8 a.m.	No 2 Section — Completed all above mentioned work. M.G. Emp⁺ semi-bombproof in Cline presented considerable difficulty as the roof had to be kept to an absolute minimum of thickness. It was arranged thus:—	
			A took 2" layers South	
			Rails to dug	
			[diagram with measurements: 1'1½", 2'9"×3" Hanover, 3 sets of 2 layers of ¼" steel plate, 8"×8", round poles]	
			Result strut under rails to keep frames apart on slant	
			C.R. Cheney Capt⁺ OC Relays	

Army Form C. 2118.

WAR DIARY
or
INTELLIGENCE SUMMARY. 7 bz Cy R.E.

(Erase heading not required.)

Instructions regarding War Diaries and Intelligence Summaries are contained in F. S. Regs., Part II. and the Staff Manual respectively. Title pages will be prepared in manuscript.

Place	Date	Hour	Summary of Events and Information	Remarks and references to Appendices
	7/9/16	8 a.m.	No 3 Section Completed officers sleeping room dugout. Also 4 entrance dugout. Proceeded with tunnelling for M.G. Emplt in front of M 30. Commenced N.G. Emplacement in H.S. line Sketches follow next month. Commenced M.G. Emplacement at junction HAVANNAH with H.S. line. Sketch follows next week.	
			No 4 Section Moved up to ARRAS to relieve No 2.	
			No 1 Section as before.	
			No 2 Section Returned to DAINVILLE.	
	8/9/16	8 a.m.	SUCRERIE. Continued Fumo-Crente M.G. Emplacement at ACHICOURT.	
			No 4 Section Commenced M.G. Emplacement at CHATEAU RONVILLE Continued mined dugout left from previous month for M.G. splinterproof Emplt in H.S. line on scheme left. Commenced mined dugouts B line, left of RONVILLE Commenced mined dugout for M.G. Emplt C line.	CR Crawley Capt. OC 62Cy.RE
			Nos 1 & 2 as before.	
	14/9/16	8 a.m.	No 1 Section moved up to ARRAS to take over from No 3 which returned to DAINVILLE. No 3 took on mined dugout for Clair Emplt. No 2 Section Continued ACHICOURT Emplt. Remainder moved to BERNEVILLE to continue work being done by No 1 Section — chiefly completion water supply including second entrance & tunnels. Branching on along 2 scales in both DAINVILLE & BERNEVILLE inkings closed. Stored materials gathered together in being used up.	

1577 Wt. W10791/1773 500,000 1/15 D. D. & L. A.D.S.S./Forms/C. 2118.

WAR DIARY
or
INTELLIGENCE SUMMARY. 1/62 Coy, R.E.

Army Form C. 2118.

Place	Date	Hour	Summary of Events and Information	Remarks and references to Appendices
DAINVILLE	21/5/16	8a.m.	No. 1 Section. Completed one side M.G. emplt in front of H.30. Commenced tunnelling on other side of road & produces another emplt & fire on other side. Sketches of work as finally completed follow:— [sketches with annotations: "bank of road", "hollow", "10' thick over", "H.30 Front line trench", "main tunnel 6'×3', 60' long", "12'", "¼" steel plates carrying sods only", "loophole", "2'6" about", "4'", "1'", "recessed roof put over"] Note: All work was done from inside, so that surface was not touched except for loophole & air shaft down mine. Object being to flank front line wire & be in cover from Shrapnel. Recess cut on right for No. 2 Reconn after trans. Road ACHICOURT to BEAURAINS.	C.R. Gurney Capt. OC. 1/62 Coy. N.

Army Form C. 2118.

WAR DIARY
or
INTELLIGENCE SUMMARY. of 62 Coy. R.E.
(Erase heading not required.)

Place	Date	Hour	Summary of Events and Information	Remarks and references to Appendices
	21/9/16	8 am	No 4 Section. Completed laying of tram line for taking materials to dugout at CHATEAU, RONVILLE. Preparing win etc. for same. Remainder proceeding with work as above. ACHICOURT Sept: [sketch with labels: "wall of house 1'6\"", "4\" air space", "18\"", "9\"", "18\"", "air space", "9\" air space", "rails touching", "7'", "(10' other way)", "A B C D", "layer reinforcement anything available", "layer reinforcement anything available"] A, B, C, D iron bars 1", 9" apart strengthened with expanded metal pieces of 2 in T iron etc, as available.	

C.H.R. Chaney
Capt R.E.
OC 62 Coy RE

WAR DIARY
or
INTELLIGENCE SUMMARY
Army Form C. 2118.

of 62 Coy R.E.

Place	Date	Hour	Summary of Events and Information	Remarks and references to Appendices
DAINVILLE	2/5/16	8 a.m.	**No 4 Section** – Mixed dugout for splinter proof dugout on left of R.E. line. M.G. Emplacement (Iron Concrete) at CHATEAU, RONVILLE. Sketches follow. Knocked off work and parts of B line in order to concentrate on this M.G. Empl. as above.	
			No 2 Section – moved into DAINVILLE. Commenced with an advanced Dressing Station RUE DE BAC(?) ARRAS. Chasing cellar connecting same together – putting down new floor being 9" airspace above cellar. Top flooring of this floor put on between Inside layer 18" thick. Making 12 Bangalore torpedoes. Commenced shot mat for M.G. Emplacement but method splinterproof. Sketches follow. Achicourt H.S. Emplacement. 2 Min., HAUTEVILLE Trench School.	
			No 3 Section – All mixed entrance scars. Intermittently running 2 Enquiries. WARLUS. How to stop. LIENCOURT making Lids for Dirt Restraint. BERNEVILLE. Work on mixed dugout for M.G. Empl. C line.	
			No 1 Section – M.G. Emplacements in front of H30. Sketches. Work as found necessary to complete fitter M.G. Emplacements R.S. Line + Haravensh. Sketches follow.	
	3/5/16	6 a.m.	All working as before.	Capt. O.C. 62 Coy R.E.

D.A.A.G.
3rd Echelon.

Herewith War Diary of 62nd Field Coy R.E. for period of 1st June to 30 June 1916.

Please acknowledge receipt.

C.H.R. Chrovey
Capt R.E.
Commanding 62nd (Field) Co. R.E.

June.
Vol 10
Army Form C. 2118.

XIV
62 Coy. R.E.

WAR DIARY
or
INTELLIGENCE SUMMARY
(Erase heading not required.)

Place	Date	Hour	Summary of Events and Information	Remarks and references to Appendices
DAINVILLE	7/6/18	8 a.m.	**No. 4 Section.** Completed mined dug out for flint proof M.G. Emplacement M.S. line. Drawings attached. Emplacement improved by saturating earth over roof with drainings). M.G. Emplacement CHATEAU, RONVILLE proceeding. Commenced provision of roofs of 4 tubes of no galvd. to HAVANNAH, HAVELOCK & HAIG Streets. Also waterproofing pipe line for same from fresh supply in ARRAS. **No. 1 Section.** Proceeding with M.G. Emplacements H.30. Havannah, & M.S. (junction with HAYMARKET) **No. 2 Section.** Proceeding with construction of dressing station RUE DE BUCQUOY, ARRAS. Air shafts made on a cellar roof by means of pistols 9" Mors ≡ 3'6" 9 endings 3'.6" 9" endings underground as a second exit made 6 with brick rubble. Cellars connected together underground as a second exit made to street. Completed M.G. Emplacement ACHICOURT with erection of small lantern roof for same. Drawings attached. Bangalor Topedoes continuing. Steel roof for M.G. Emplacement HAVANNAH proceeding. Position for new M.G. Emplacement ACHICOURT recommended, & also positions for 7 O.P's & relays for infantry in the trenches.	C.H.R. Chaney Capt R.E OC 62 Coy

WAR DIARY or INTELLIGENCE SUMMARY of 62 Coy. R.E.

Army Form C. 2118.

Place	Date	Hour	Summary of Events and Information	Remarks and references to Appendices
DAINVILLE	16/6/16	8 a.m.	No. 3 Section. Completed work on mined dugout for M.G. Sergt. C. line. Now strengthened surface-ment by putting extra roof over 18" thick had chalk covered on 6" of loose thickly making a 6" air space. The growth of grass enabled this to be done which could not have been done before. Remainder, BERNEVILLE, WARLUS, LIENCOURT.	
	17/6/16	8 a.m.	No. 4 Section. Completed M.G. Emplacement CHATEAU, RONVILLE, work in tracing up left & do & taking up of from line, for which 2 or 5 men would be required for a while. Drawings attached. Returned to DAINVILLE.	
			No. 3 Section. Hand up to ARRAS. Commenced 4 shafts for mined dugouts in H.S. line not of HEYSAS & in HEYSAS itself. 2 men used for superintending in O.P. dump.	
			No. 1 Section. Completed M.G. Emplacements #30 A.S. (junction with HAYMARKET) & HAWANNAH. (Drawings attached) work in tracing up left & do for which 2 or 3 men at each emplacement were required for a while.	Capt. Cresswell Captain
			No. 2 Section. Put up steel roof over HAVANNAH emplacement. Proceeded with drawing station RUE DE BUCQUOY. Constructed 4 bridges on ACHICOURT-BEAURAINS road over trenches to carry 6cwt heavy lorries. Also 2 on ACHICOURT–RONVILLE & RUE DE BUCQUOY. Commenced accumulation of stores for new emplacement ACHICOURT. Moved up to ARRAS.	

WAR DIARY
or
INTELLIGENCE SUMMARY

Army Form C. 2118.

62 Coy. R.E.

(Erase heading not required.)

Instructions regarding War Diaries and Intelligence Summaries are contained in F.S. Regs., Part II. and the Staff Manual respectively. Title Pages will be prepared in manuscript.

Place	Date	Hour	Summary of Events and Information	Remarks and references to Appendices
DAINVILLE	19/6/16	8 a.m.	No. 4 Section. 4 men sent night to CHATEAU Emplacement, RONVILLE finishing up. 4 men to assist No. 3 Section on dug-outs H.S. line. 6 on Listening Post. Special operation in conjunction with small party 9 KRR's 'flaming' up MAISON ISOLEE in Somme line. Remainder old jobs.	
			No. 2 Section. New M.G. Emplacement (No. 2) ACHICOURT. Completed another 3 bridges over trenches fronting houses in RUE DE BUCQUOY. Proceeded as all times with preparation of O.P. posts. Finished O.P. post for R.A. ACHICOURT. Completed mine shaft for Commenced work on O.P. post for R.E. in DAINVILLE. 3 Men installed & sunk a pump to BERNEVILLE dug-out for R.E. as before.	
			No. 3 Section.	
	30/6/16	8 a.m.	Period active. Small parties detailed much preparation for taking part in various raids on enemy lines which did not come off. No. 3 Section. Dug-outs H.S. & M.S. lines (mainly) interfered with by stratum of water. No. 2 Section. M.G. Emplacement ACHICOURT & B.H.Q. O.P. posts in line for infantry. 2 further bridges W. of DE BUCQUOY. No. 1 Section. Finished O.P. for R.A. ACHICOURT. Assisted R.E. with shelter for wounded at railway 2 bridges RUE DE CANTORNA Emplacement for mg between ACHICOURT & RN NY + alongside HAVANNAH track between BERNEVILLE / ST SAUVEUR. No. 4 Section. Assisted No. 3 with dugouts. RA with dugouts, railway embankment DAINVILLE. RA gun platforms. Constructed gstores in the R.E. Pall. Preparation of stores.	C.R. Livery Cpt 1/7/16 O.C. 62 Coy RE.

62 J.C.R.S.
appt to Vol 10
June.

XV

D.A.G. G.H.Q. 3rd Echelon

I regret to state that the drawings in my War Diary for month of June are incorrect.
They should be amended as follows
M.G. Emplacement
Chateau Rouville.   Left hand bottom corner reads
"Small scale plan & section showing position of proposed dug out under emplacement."
"This M.G emplacement is ~~100~~ 150 yards behind our front line of trenches."
~~in open ground~~   under heading

Emplacement in H.S. line
under this heading following words
This emplacement is ~~—~~ 70 yds behind the front line.

C.H.R. Chesney
Major R.E.
Commanding 62nd (Field) Co. R.E.

16-7-16

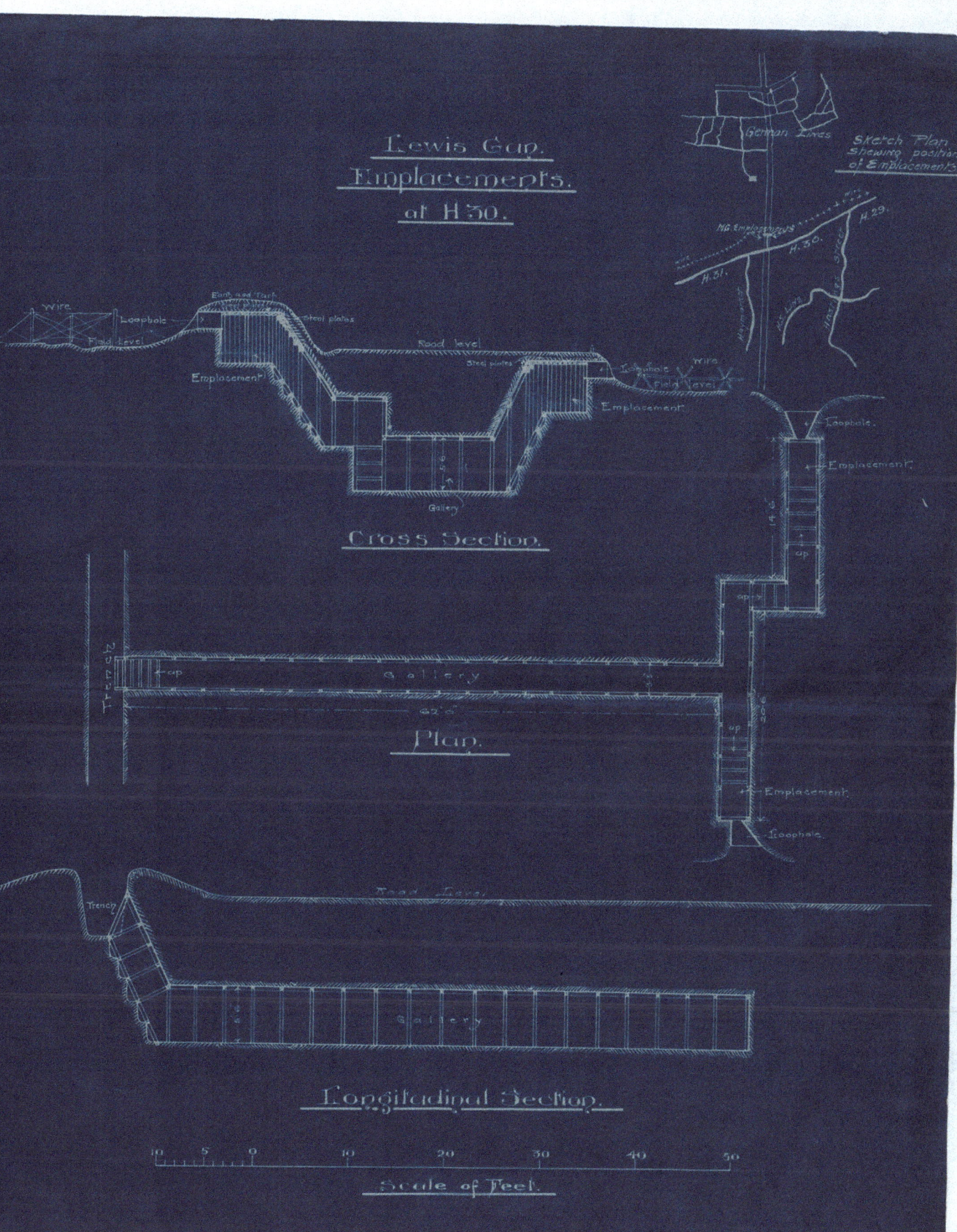

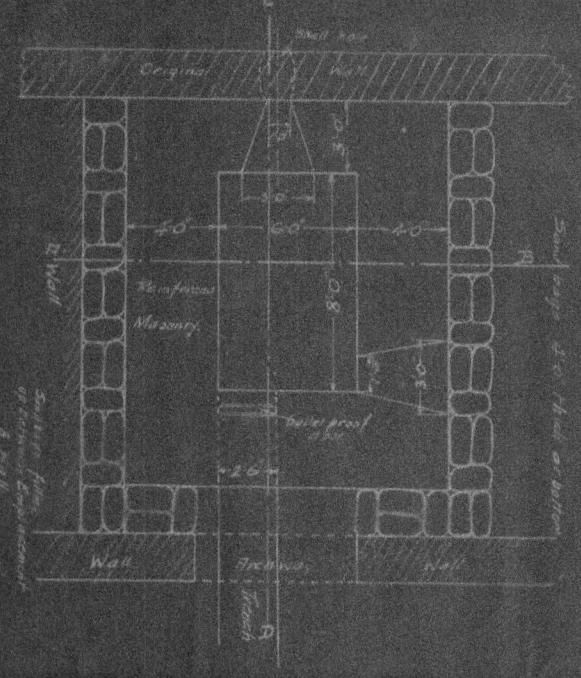

M.G. Emplacement in H.40.

Splinter proof only.

Cross Section

Plan Shewing Dugout
Scale 8 Feet to 1 inch

Plan.

Section

M.G. Emplacement in Havannah

Section. A.B.

Field Level — Havannah Trench — Trench — Gallery — Dugout

Section. C.D.

Emplacement — Loophole — Gallery

Details of Emplacement to a scale of 4 Feet to one inch.

Plan.

Gun Platform — Loophole — Ladder

Section.

Brushwood & Grass Mats — Loophole — Gun Platform

Plan.

Havannah Trench — Loophole — Gun Platform — Emplacement — Gallery — Dugout — Trench

12.6
14.6

Scale of Feet.

0 5 10 20 30 40

Army Form C. 2118.

14 July
172 Coy R.E.
Vol 11

WAR DIARY
or
INTELLIGENCE SUMMARY
(Erase heading not required.)

Place	Date	Hour	Summary of Events and Information	Remarks and references to Appendices
DAINVILLE	9/7/16	8 a.m.	No 3 Section. An inclined dugout in H.S. & H.B. lines. 2 sets in H.S. completed rough plan. [sketch] 15' solid ground above. connecting tunnel arched in the chalk. Sandbags taken out and to first branch H.S. line. Trench very few. [sketch with dimensions 3', 2'6", 6'6", Struts, plank frontage] ¼ repeated where? All timbers 3"x3". The entry galleries will in future be constructed down a little further than the connecting galleries so as to form their own stops. 20.. Infantry attached on 8/7/16. 9/0 more on 8/7/16. No 2 Section. Doing T.O.P. in H.S. line. Sketches & standardized articles attached. Iron covers are made in foundry in ARRAS by this section. M.G.E.n.M. in ACMICOD RT.	C.R.P Chaney Major. O.C. 172 Coy R.E.

Army Form C. 2118.

WAR DIARY
or
INTELLIGENCE SUMMARY   62 Coy. R.E.

(Erase heading not required.)

Place	Date	Hour	Summary of Events and Information	Remarks and references to Appendices
DANVILLE	9/7/16	8 a.m.	**No 1 Section.** Helping R.M.E. with shelters at Railway Embankment ACHICOURT & tunnelled shelter 4'x4' in back dugouts RAVANNAH. Repaired stand of N°30 emplacement which was somewhat damaged by heavy trench mortar shell though not seriously. Made frames for mined dugouts in Park. Moved up to AREAS to work on mine crater under O.C. 29 Coy.R.E. on 8/7/16 evening.	
			No. 4 Section Continued construction of gun platforms for R.A. Sketches attached. Helped R.A. with dugouts RAILWAY CUTTING, DANVILLE. Worked on Y.M.C.A. hut DANVILLE. Worked on sound ranging apparatus for R.A. Made frames for mined dugouts for N° 3 Section. Repaired frontline trench from CHATEAU RONVILLE line at junction with HOLBORN. Laid 160 yards trench line at junction with W.B. line. Laid 480 yards tramline from RUE DE BUC & VOY parallel to RAVANNAH up to its junction with W.B. line.	
14/7/16		8 a.m.	**N° 4 Section** Moved up to AREAS & relief N° 3. Started a 3 some mined dugout in W.B. line near HAVANNAH. Also 3 tank Mortar positions, improvements required in the slope of tunnels above the mortars might fire.	
			N° 3 Section. Had to leave the 3 some dugout at N° 3 not detailed & complete store dugouts later. Kitchen W. is detailed & complete store dugouts later. 2 some dugout in W.B. line is returned to DANVILLE	

WAR DIARY
or
INTELLIGENCE SUMMARY 6/4/16 R.E.

Army Form C. 2118.

Place	Date	Hour	Summary of Events and Information	Remarks and references to Appendices
DAINVILLE	16/7/16	8 a.m.	No. 2 Section completed 6 O.P.'s & Inf's in line. Presented transport tunnel H.30 which was slightly damaged by French Mortars. Improve an entrance & a dugout in H.B. in night. Made an iron door and safety plate plates for M.G. Supt. CHATEAU RONVILLE. No. 4 Section Adv in DAINVILLE No. 3 Section Y.M.C.A. WANQUETIN made nine frames & odd jobs for line.	1 Sgt killed etc etc 1 Sapper etc. wounded etc etc
	23/7/16	8 a.m.	No. 2 Section went to Inspelling war WANQUETIN for training. Cy. took over I sector left. Headed over to Brector to the Hospice. Cy. headed on I sector right relief 1/6 2nd Lghs. moved to BREWERIERE, WANQUETIN.	
	25/7/16	8 a.m.	Cy. moved to IVERGNY.	
	29/7/16	8 a.m.	Cy. moved to BARLY.	
	30/7/16	8 a.m.	Cy. moved to BARLY.	
	31/7/16	8 a.m.	Cy. into BARLY.	

C.R. Cheney
Capt.
O. i/c 1/2 Coy R.E.

31/7/16

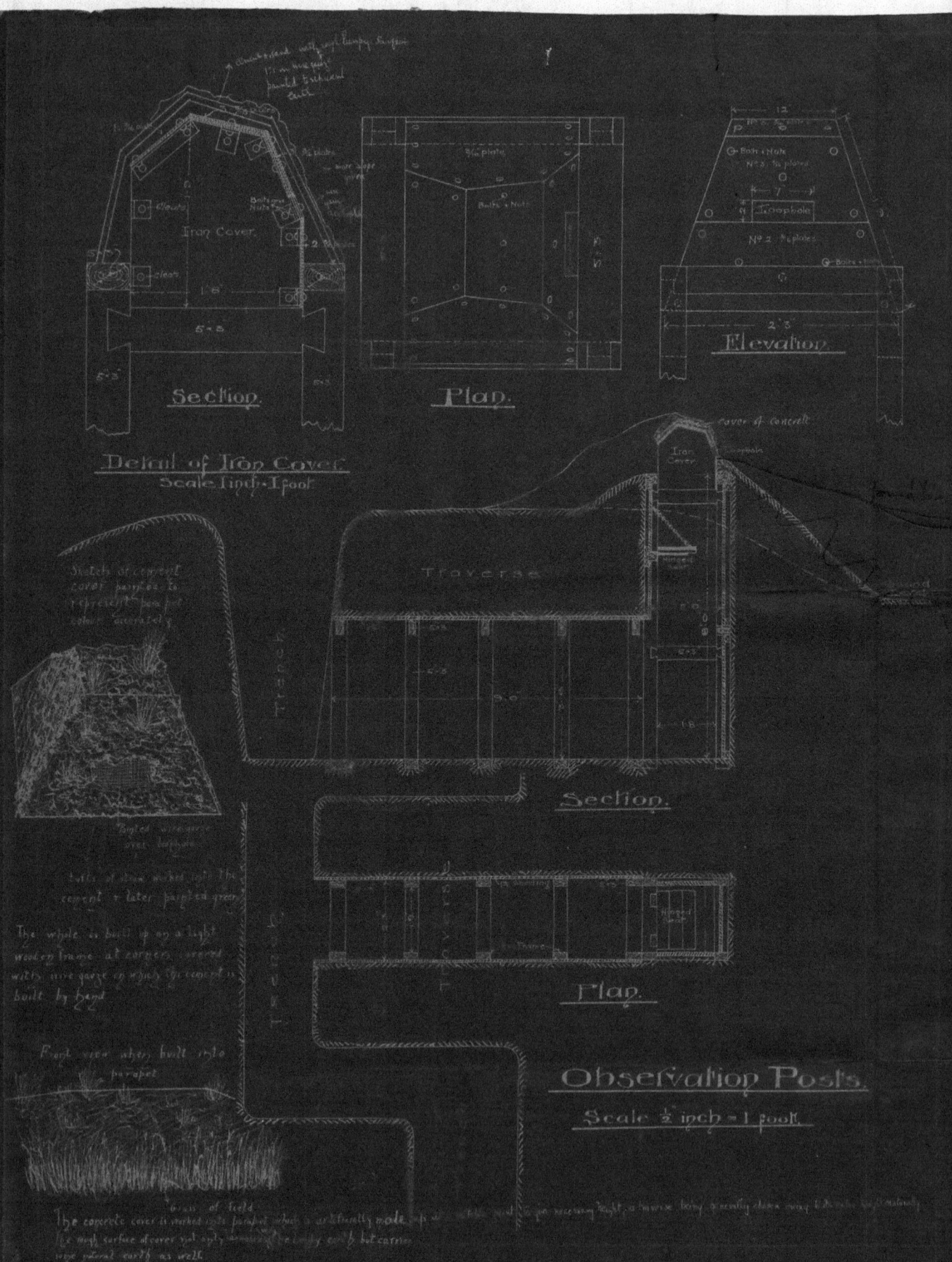

<u>14th Division.</u>

<u>62nd FIELD COMPANY</u>

<u>ROYAL ENGINEERS</u>

<u>A U G U S T   1 9 1 6</u>

Attached: Report on Operations.

CRE 14th Divn.

I have the following points to report with reference to the recent operations.
I am reporting from an RE point of view entirely.

The whole question of success in the construction of these strong points hangs on the simple fact whether the infantry have got a protecting screen out or not.

In the centre Diana point was constructed exactly as intended. The trench was good & the wire was good. Casualties were slight & due more to misfortune than any deliberate intention on the enemy's part.

In this case the screen consisted of the new line being dug in front of the ORCHARD TRENCH.

On the left, (una Capt (or Major) MAXWELL had the situation so well in hand that although the strong point was constructed on the extreme left flank of our front line

yet we could work without interruption
Result, no casualties & the work was
got through with despatch.
But this was due entirely to Capt
Maxwell's enterprise Scan. Some Germans
crept up during the night in shell holes
& fired 15 snipt or bomb our men
wiring. Capt Maxwell's men immediately
set about them & we had no more trouble
getting the job through without difficulty
Lt. Kilby was responsible for the efficient
clearing of ground in our immediate
front.
On the right however the situation was
entirely different. See sketch plan:

The Liverpools were struggling to connect
up the trench from A to B being sniped
at from the immediate right front in
DELVILLE WOOD.
Bombs were also being thrown at them
They had lost a large number of their
men
On the arrival of the R E officer &
wiring parties it was found impossible
to show a hand above the parapet from
A to D. Any sign of movement would
bring 6 to 8 bullets at the person
moving.

My officer cleared up the situation a little & laid out a trench to be dug from C to D, but before he could see the work completed he was hit.

The R.E. party was at a loss to know what to do - there was not room for them to work from C to D besides the Liverpools working party. They set about finding ammunition, grenades & a lost Lewis gun. A Lewis gun (Liverpools) was installed at C & the lost one with ammunition was returned to the infantry.

It is to be realised that the sappers got out to work at C but were bombed. They were then ordered to get into the trench & stand to by the Infantry officer as a bombing attack was feared.

This is a clear example I think, of the impossibility of getting a party of 75, as our party was, on to constructing a strong point unless there is a screen covering them

Either there must be a screen or else the infantry outposts have succeeded in driving the enemy's snipers &

bombers to arms length to give room for work.

In this case we were actually trying to construct a strong point in amongst the line of outposts.

Therefore I think the lesson for R.E. is that if the garrison cannot guarantee that the enemy are kept out of bombing distance then the strong point must be constructed behind the line taken up.

For this reason the orders given us as regards the siting of strong points should be elastic & should read "in the neighbourhood of .... behind the furthest line taken up by the infantry after the assault".

A point infantry officers do not realise is that the wire around a point constructed to hold a garrison of 15 men only would generally measure some 120 yards wide by 80 yds deep.

That means one must have clear room for 200 yards by 160 yds taking

40 yards as bombing distance.

All the difficulties & arguments arising between the R.E. & infantry on the matter of the construction of these strong points arises from the lack of recognition of this point i.e. of dimensions.

I think it is a matter that should be circularised to all so that a right conception of the whole matter may be the foundation of future efforts.

19/8/16

C.R. Creagh
Capt R.E.
Commanding 62nd (Field) Co. R.E.

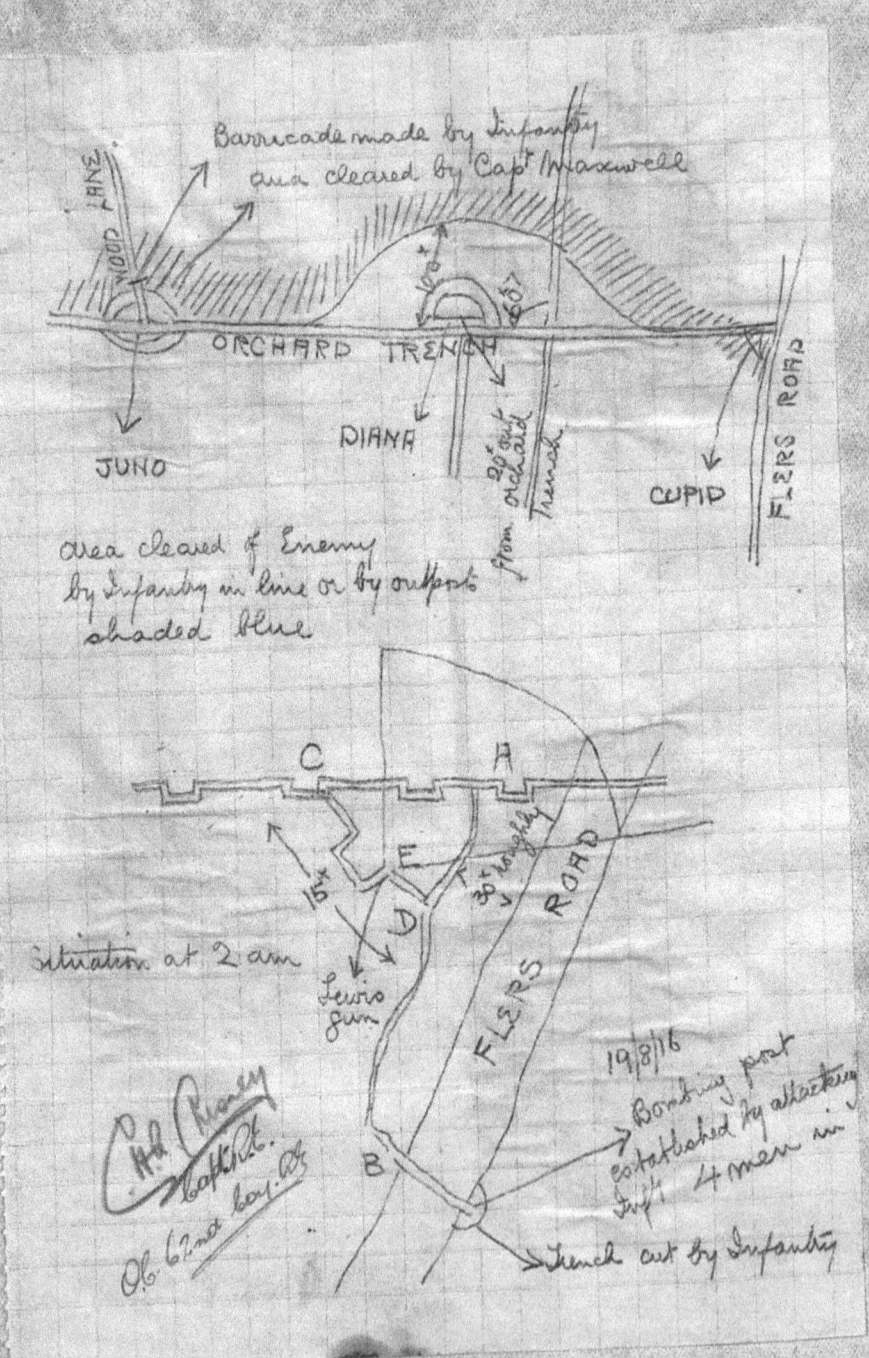

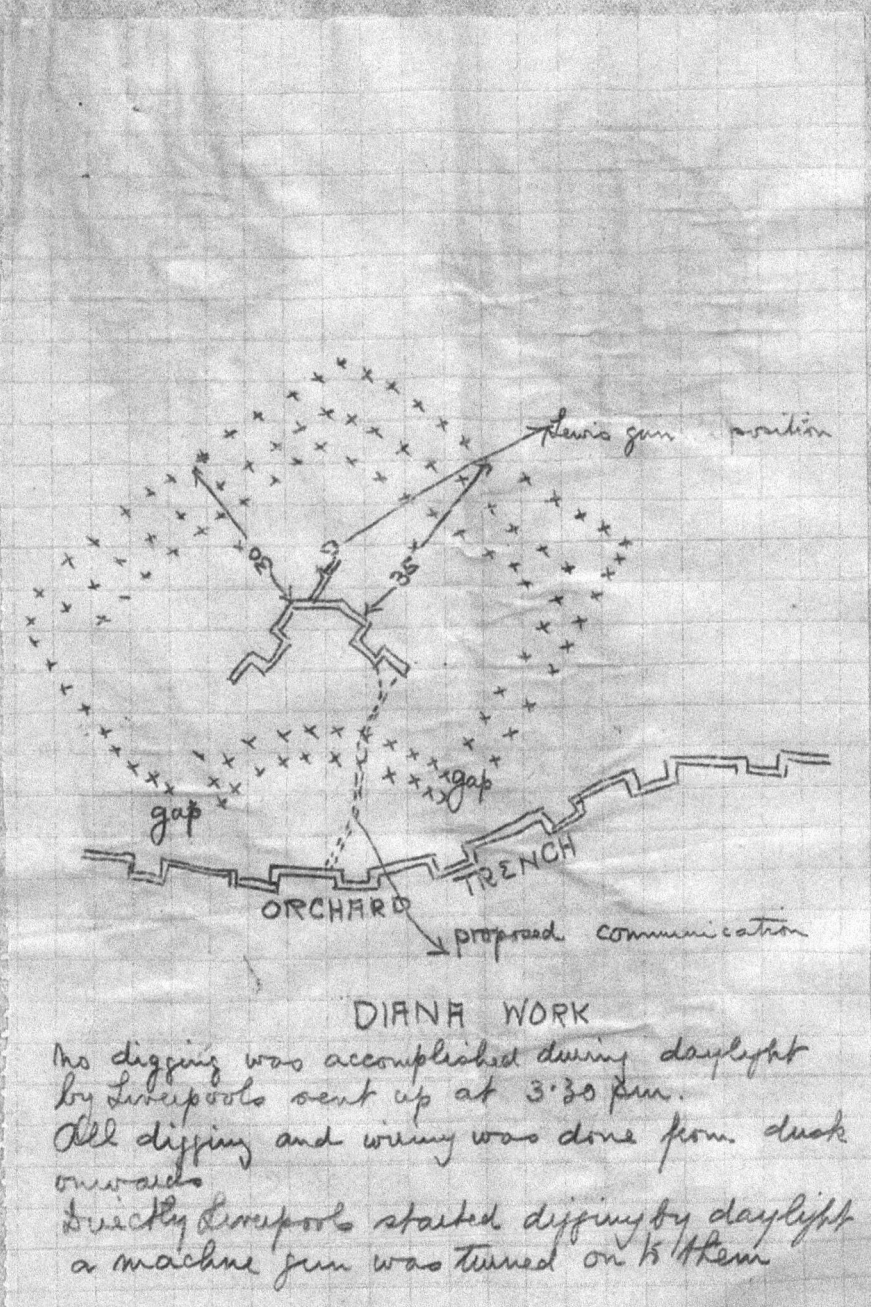

DIANA WORK

No digging was accomplished during daylight by Liverpools sent up at 3.30 pm.

All digging and wiring was done from dusk onwards.

Directly Liverpools started digging by daylight a machine gun was turned on to them.

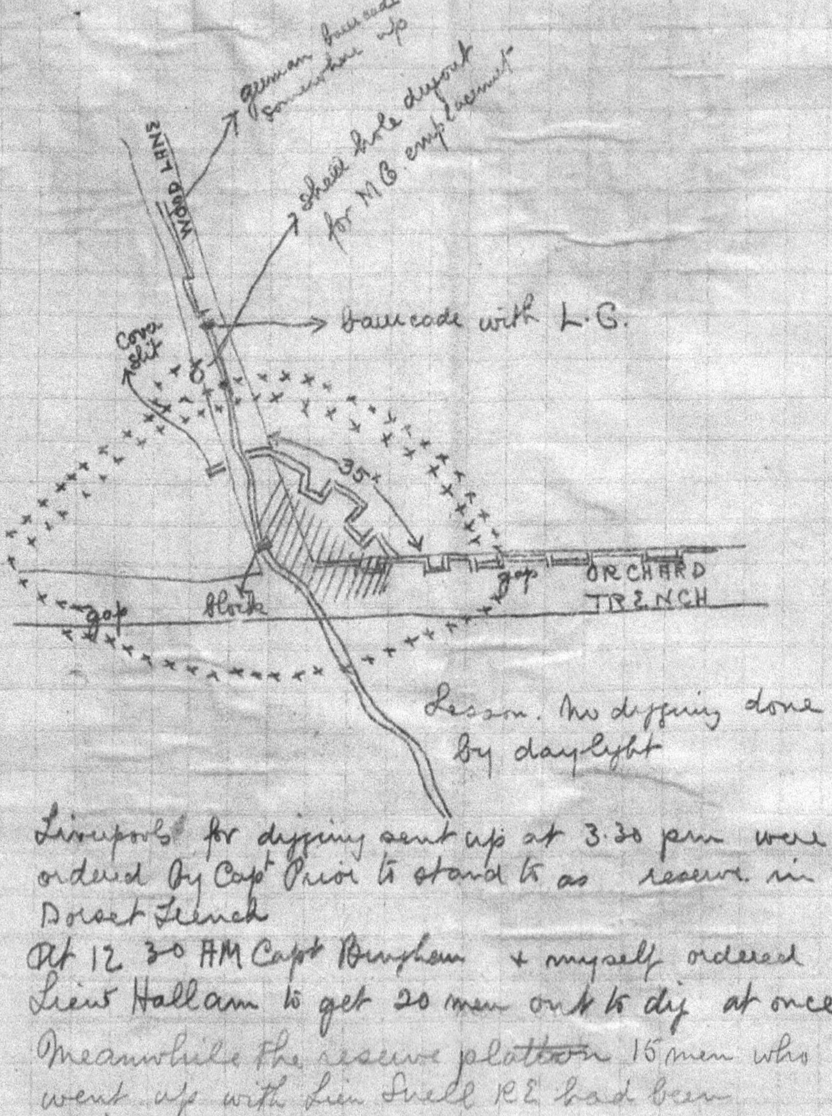
German barricade somewhere up
WOOD LANE
shell hole dugout for M.G. emplacement
barricade with L.G.
Cover slit
35×
gap
Block
gap
ORCHARD TRENCH
Lesson. No digging done by daylight

Liverpools for digging sent up at 3.30 pm were ordered by Capt Prior to stand to as reserve in Dorset Trench

At 12.30 AM Capt Bingham & myself ordered Lieut Hallam to get 20 men out to dig at once

Meanwhile the reserve ~~platoon~~ 15 men who went up with Lieu Snell R.E. had been digging.

WAR DIARY or INTELLIGENCE SUMMARY

62 Coy. R.E.

(Erase heading not required.)

Instructions regarding War Diaries and Intelligence Summaries are contained in F.S. Regs., Part II. and the Staff Manual respectively. Title Pages will be prepared in manuscript.

Place	Date	Hour	Summary of Events and Information	Remarks and references to Appendices
	1/8/16	8 a.m.	Coy. marched to ST HILAIRE	
	7/8/16	8 a.m.	Rested ST HILAIRE. Training, mining, machine etc., Transport work on L. de C.	
	8/8/16	8 a.m.	Returned CANDAS to HERICOURT billeted in BURE-SUR-ANCRE	
	12/8/16	8 a.m.	Rested BURE-SUR-ANCRE. Recon. officers sent up to the line to take over 93rd Fd Coy. sector 2 off. 1 N.C.O.	
	13/8/16	8 a.m.	No. 1 & 2 Sections 200 yards away from S18.8.6 to S18.8.7.5. Shest S17.c.S.w. LONGUEVAL Sh57c. Sh36s2. 3 no consolidating Roman cut line S18.B.5.2.	
	14/8/16	8 a.m.	1&2 laying out reconstructing new communication trench S18.c.9.2½ to S18.c.Y.R.1½ with no Infantry. 3 no on CARLTON TRENCH on kfm. S16.B.9.5.	
	15/8/16	8 a.m.	1&2 no kfm with no Infantry. 3 no as kfm.	
	16/8/16	8 a.m.	1&2 no kfm with no Infantry, completed trench. Commenced new one S14.c.1.2 to S10.D.9½.½. 3 no as kfm.	
	17/8/16	8 a.m.	3 ra taking up mining stores with 20 parties for strong points in future attack. 2 artillery trench completed started. Parts (3rd lot) tramrails completed. 4 No fm made by 14th pn up for Arty. to new trenches.	
	18/8/16	8 a.m.	1 & 2 making shght 15/17 G attack by 4th G. Bde on ORCHARD TRENCH successful. 2 strong points made, and unsuccessful. Special report attached. Coy. Resting.	2 officers 1 N.C.O. 11 R.E. O.R. 2 No. 15 P 2 no as 15 P
	20/8/16	8 a.m.	No. 2 with Green making R.M. O.P. near LONGUEVAL. S.11.D.7.2.	
	21/8/16	8 a.m.	Reconnoitre 12 no with 15 no on Communication trench S.11.D.7.2 to S.17.D.6.7.	

WAR DIARY or INTELLIGENCE SUMMARY

62 Coy R.E.

Place	Date	Hour	Summary of Events and Information	Remarks and references to Appendices
In the Field	22/8/16	8 a.m.	1, 2, 3 & 4 Sections on shifts making Batt'n H'drs. dugouts at S.15.c.5.3	
	23/8/16	8 a.m.	do	
	24/8/16	8 a.m.	do finished 4 p.m. 25/8/16	
			2 roofs, top on 5"x3" girders supported by 5" mail space + hurdle wire	
	25/8/16	8 a.m.	Quieter nt'p. Blt previous evening. Unsuccessful. No opportunity done R.E. on strong points. Workstation. 10 men noted no guides + unfrequent gnng up. Stokes Mortar bombs urgently required.	
	26/8/16	8 a.m.	Day 40 men carried up improvement of French T.B.C. 4.9½. to T.13.a.5.3. Heavy shelling. No 3 Section working on with 2 officers laying out new trenches in front. Unsuccessful owing	
			No 1 Section 10 men to shelling causing withdrawal of covering party.	
	27/8/16	8 a.m.	Coy resting.	
	28/8/16	8 a.m.	1 officer & 8 men of No 1 cutting road at MERICOURT. Quieter than 2 men. Making frames for wire cloth knife rests. 12 men. Making Lune - Conflans 6 mm.	
	29/8/16	8 a.m.	1 officer to men cutting road. 12 mm making frames. 16 mm making bone traps.	
	30/8/16	8 a.m.	as above. Raid completed	
DERNANCOURT	31/8/16	8 a.m.	16 mm making horse frames. 24 mm out to MERICOURT & future pontoon bar for the march.	

Coy arrived by road to DERNANCOURT
Coy. harnessed on R. & A. Forms/C.2118/12

E. C. Connery Capt
OC 62 Coy R.E.

Army Form C. 2118.

WAR DIARY or INTELLIGENCE SUMMARY

62 Co. R.E. Vol 13

(Erase heading not required.)

Place	Date	Hour	Summary of Events and Information	Remarks and references to Appendices
	1/9/16	8 a.m.	Entrained at DERNANCOURT, detrained at AIRAINES marched to AVELESGES. Mounted branch by road.	
	2/9/16	8 a.m.	Mounted branch arrived AVELESGES 4 p.m. 1/9/16	
	3/9/16		In billets AVELESGES. Training	
	4/9/16	8 a.m.		
	5/9/16	8 a.m.	marched to VILLERS CAMPSART.	
	6/9/16	8 a.m.	Rested VILLERS CAMPSART. Training	
	7/9/16	9 a.m.	1 Officer + 25 men proceeded to AULT on the Sea for rest.	
	8/9/16		Training	
	9/9/16	10 a.m.	Rested VILLERS CAMPSART.	
	10/9/16		Section from AULT returned. Mounted Branch marched to MILLY-SUR-SOMME.	
	11/9/16	8 a.m.		
	12/9/16	8 a.m.	Co. marched to AIRAINES entrained 5.30 p.m. arrived MERICOURT 2.30 a.m. marched into billets at DERNANCOURT.	
	13/9/16	8 a.m.	Co. marched to camp FRICOURT	
	14/9/16	8 a.m.	Made camps for various units helpful in many small details in various places.	
	15/9/16			
	16/9/16	8 a.m.	Standing by during battle. One Officer & 3 wagons used for Mobile R.E. Park various parties used at various times forwarding parties etc.	
	17/9/16			
	18/9/16		Marched down to camp near BUIRE. (D.18.?)	
	19/9/16	8 a.m.	Encamped near BUIRE.	
	20/9/16	8 a.m.		

Army Form C. 2118.

WAR DIARY
or
INTELLIGENCE SUMMARY

(Erase heading not required.)

62 Coy R.E.

Place	Date	Hour	Summary of Events and Information	Remarks and references to Appendices
	20/9/16	8a.m.	In charge Major BURKE.	
	21/9/16	9a.m.	Transport marched to TALMAS. Remainder at BOIRE.	
	22/9/16	8a.m.	Transport marched to OPPY. Remainder to OPPY.	
	23/9/16	8a.m.	2 White at OPPY. No 4 Section marched to BERNEVILLE.	
	24/9/16	8a.m.	No 2 Section = BERNEVILLE. Remainder in billets OPPY.	
	25/9/16	8a.m.	No 3 Section [illegible]	
	26/9/16	8a.m.	No 4 in BERNEVILLE. Remainder marched to GOUY.	
	27/9/16	8a.m.	Maj. Coy marched to AGNY & took over line from 10 Cy R.E. with exception of No 3 Section which took over work at VARLUS. Transport at BERNEVILLE.	
	28/9/16	8a.m.	Reconnoitring trenches, improving billets & dugouts and an M.T.M. emplacements &c.	
	29/9/16	8a.m.	No 1 Section Emplacements for Heavy Trench Mortar also Tunnel Training for same. No 2. Agny Defences. No 4. Heavy Trench Mortar Emplacements also 2" Mortar Emplacements with Dugouts. Tunnel Training for same.	
	30/9/16	8a.m.	Carried on with works as on the 29/9/16. Arranged for No 4 Section to take over in Ronville Caves.	

C.H.R. Pusey
Capt.

WAR DIARY or INTELLIGENCE SUMMARY

Army Form C. 2118

Vol 14 62 Co, R.E.

Place	Date	Hour	Summary of Events and Information	Remarks and references to Appendices
In the Field	1/10/16	8 a.m.	No. 3 Section working under C.R.E. at WARLUS. No. 4 Section Heavy Trench Mortar Emplt. Left Sector Trench Tramway, making emplacements. No. 1 Section " " " Right Sector " " HYGATE STREET, improving billets. No. 2 Section Dugouts Mill Post 3. 8' disp. 2 pers. shelters unopld. Improving R.E. 4 R.S. dt. 1 billets. Improving billeting arrangements in AGNY. Making gun emplacements for dugouts.	
	2/10/16	8 a.m.	Same throughout.	
	3/10/16	8 a.m.	No. 4 Section and under arty. Trench Mortar Emplt. as R.A. did not require. Made some rifle racks. Carriers for divls. sigs, MCs for Brigade Dumps which has been taken over by Co.	
			No. 1 Section completed Improvements to billets. Commenced drainage & sunken road, making nosing traverses.	
	4/10/16	8 a.m.	In addition to above No. 1 & 2 section took over work of geo entering AGNY Front line. No. 2 Section Commenced bridge for heavy traffic on road AGNY Front line. Remainder same.	
	5/10/16	8 a.m.	No. 6 Section commenced work on Russian Sap. 3 sappers 4 & 5 Sapts to raid offso.	
	6/10/16	8 a.m.	O.C. No. 6 Section laid out advanced H. trench from G.16 A.5.20 in front of present line having to 3 sappers injured. Communication trenches from Front line to main line G.16.B.9.20, laid out by No. 6 Section officer with NCOs.	
			Remainder same.	
	7/10/16	8 a.m.	New trench in front from G.16 A.5.20 begun with infantry working parties. Remainder same as before.	
	8/10/16	8 a.m.	As above. New trench approx. 300 x in length with communication trenches about 50 x in length each side. Left Tramway laid underground in villages of AGNY about 250 x in length. Trees in trenches already dug out 150 x in length to Boyau line. Right tramway tent line from sunken road to new GATE STREET about 100 yards in length. Position between rails being laid with bricks.	1 Sapper wounded
	9/10/16	8 a.m.	As above.	

C.M. Cheney
Capt. RE
O.C. 62 Co, R.E.

WAR DIARY
or
INTELLIGENCE SUMMARY   62 Coy R.E.

(Erase heading not required.)

Army Form C. 2118.

Place	Date	Hour	Summary of Events and Information	Remarks and references to Appendices
In the field	10/10/16 11/10/16	8a.m. 8a.m.	Same as before.	
	12/10/16	8a.m.	Same as before after reputilation [?] with C.R.E.	
			No 3 Section Tramway to left shaft section. Russian Saps 13 +14. 7 saps left working Bty 150. Rifle Racks, Front camino, mining frames etc.	
			No 4 Section mining + constructing new trench. M.T.N. Emplt. not proceeded with.	
			M.T.N. Emplt. not proceeded with (dugouts being completed).	
			No.1 Section M.T.N. Emplt. near GATE STREET. Tunnel Tramway to right near GATE STREET. Drainage sinkers head with racking trenches. Gas curtains to dugouts in G.S. line. Gas curtains with No.1 Section.	
			No.2 Section Bayonets to M.G. Post. Improving tilletts in A.G.N.Y. Making shug at frames for M.G. 6fpr.	
	13/10/16	8a.m.	As above. Russian sap No.15 thing carried on by No.4 Section.	
			No.2 Section making a redout frame stand.	
	14/10/16 15/10/16 16/10/16	8a.m. 8a.m. 8a.m.	As above.	
			No.4 Section Commenced making trackstops in nosetunnel.	
	17/10/16 18/10/16	8a.m. 8a.m.	All progress on Russian saps stopped. Commenced making two deme [?] trench with hopholed barricade to stop. heavy carrying up saps.	
	19/10/16	8a.m.	Trench under road between G.12 + G.13 blown in. No 4 Section tooh in hand repair strengthening & plans.	

Army Form C. 2118.

WAR DIARY or INTELLIGENCE SUMMARY 62 Coy RE.

(Erase heading not required.)

Instructions regarding War Diaries and Intelligence Summaries are contained in F.S. Regs., Part II. and the Staff Manual respectively. Title Pages will be prepared in manuscript.

Place	Date	Hour	Summary of Events and Information	Remarks and references to Appendices
In the field	20/10/16	8 a.m.	As above. No 3 Section changed duties with No 6 Section, having changed over on previous day.	
	21/10/16	8 a.m.	1, 2, + 3 Sections majority of men had a day off & paraded for baths.	
	22/10/16	8 a.m.	No 2 Section commenced interior improvement of left tramway to junction GRAVEL STREET – namma line.	
	23/10/16	8 a.m.	Do as above – Stores barricades & firing blocks completed in 5 houses supporting station of which one stopped.	
	24/10/16	8 a.m.	No 3 Section commenced putting out a further line fine in front of present front, ie a line of strong points inside the middle line of front line.	
	25/10/16	8 a.m.	O.C. Sperid Bde RE commenced reconnaissance of front to install atone of new front line to work infantry.	
	26/10/16	8 a.m.	– do – had worked an average depth of 16 ft. It was found preferable to do this filthy saulding rather than any other part, trusting to daylight. Men work in parties by day filling sandbags within hunt and the parts in front of the night in shifts. These were than used in infantry in filling to new front line. (horses for gas cylinders) No 3 Section commenced putting in new front steps. Cross first stops.	
	27/10/16	8 a.m.	Nos 1, 2, & 3 Sections each had 15 men on installation of new front line. Remainder. One certain bayonets sunken road strengthening retrenchments, gas cyl. Mill Post dugouts complete. ground kept (buried in water)	
			No 1 " Improvement of left tramway line.	
			No 2 " " " "	
			No 3 " " (improved stepping station site.)	
	28/10/16	8 a.m.	Nos 1, 2, 3 Sections + 150 Special RE. carried on with installation of new strong point line. "
No 1 Section remainder. On certain bayonets sunken and retrieving + Sting theory
No 2 " Improvement of left tramway line a screen of tramp
No 3 " New Trench, deepening + running shaft by night.	
	29/10/16	8 a.m.	Same as work on 28th inst.	
	30/10/16	"	Same as work on 27th	
	31/10/16			

2449 Wt W14957/M90 750,000 1/16 J.B.C. & A. Forms/C.2118/12

Army Form C. 2118.

WAR DIARY
or
INTELLIGENCE SUMMARY.
(Erase heading not required.)

Vol 15

Confidential.

War Diary
of
62nd Bde R.F.A.
From 1st November 1916 to 30th November 1916.

(Volume I)

Army Form C. 2118.

WAR DIARY
or
INTELLIGENCE SUMMARY

(Erase heading not required.)

Instructions regarding War Diaries and Intelligence Summaries are contained in F. S. Regs., Part II. and the Staff Manual respectively. Title Pages will be prepared in manuscript.

62nd COMPANY ROYAL ENGINEERS

Place	Date	Hour	Summary of Events and Information	Remarks and references to Appendices
In the Field	1-11-16	8 am	Nos 1, 2 & 3 Sections took het 13 men on new pattern firesteps	
			No 1 Remainder - gas curtains - dugouts - sunken road	
			No 2 " - improvement of tramway line - Mill post dugouts - gas curtains	
			No 3 " - New French Gry - T.M. emplacements	
			4 Reinforcements to billets in 146 Brigade area	
	2-11-16		Same as above	
	3-11-16		do	
	4-11-16		do - Handed out work on loan to 70th Field Coy RE	
	5-11-16	12 noon	Marched to Savy 12 noon - arrived 6 pm. No 4 Section to Izbaway	
	6-11-16	8 am	" Rested 6 am " 1 pm	
	7-11-16	8 am	Training	
	8-11-16	8 "	do - No 3 Section moved to Lencourt	
	9-11-16	8 "	do	
	10-11-16	11 am	Remainder of Company, Transport et noted to IVERGNY	
	11-11-6	8 am	Training, No 3 & 4 sec bunking, RE Dump. at Le Canay & Lioncourt	
	12-11-16	"	do	
	16-11-16	"	do	
	18-11-16	"	do - Nos 1 & 2 Sections relieve 3 & 4 Sections. Capt. Clancy transferred to Senior Officers	
	21-11-16		do - Took out Labout workshops from 61st Bay.	
	23-11-16		W. E. Coy - formed in Coy	
	25-11-16		do	
	27-11-16	"	Whole Company working on surrounding villages, bunking, horse troughs, etc.	
	28-11-16	2 p	No 3 moved to GRAND RULLECOURT	
	29-11-16	8 am	Working on surrounding villages	
	30-11-6	"	do	

(S) Keen Capt. R.E.
Commanding 62nd (Field) Co. R.E

WAR DIARY
or
INTELLIGENCE SUMMARY

Army Form C. 2118.

62nd C R.E
Vol 16

Place	Date	Hour	Summary of Events and Information	Remarks and references to Appendices
In the Field	1-12-16		Company in Rest Area. Working on surrounding villages, bunking, horse troughs etc. No 1 Section at IVERGNY training. No 2 " - LIENCOURT hunting etc. No 3 " - GRAND RULLECOURT " No 4 " - Workshops LARBRET & SOMBRIN	
"	6-12-16		do	3 OR Killed 6 wounded
"	12-12-16		do	
"	14-12-16		Company assembled at HQ IVERGNY	
"	15-12-16		" moved to SIMENCOURT	
"	16-12-16		Commenced work in line	1 st Lymn Transfd to 3rd F.S. cay
"	17-12-16		" AGNY, No 1 Section & Transport at WARLUS. Look over from 10% Field Coy RE	
"	18-12-16		No 1 Sect hutting etc at WARLUS No 2 Dugouts in GOAT POST, & GIRL ST & G5.11. Trench tramway No 3 MG Empl. 46, Empl No F Dugout G21 & G19 No 4 Dugouts, LHS Row St, B3a. Dumps in Sunken Road	
"	20-12-16		No 4 finished repairs to dump in Sunken Road	
"	24-12-16		No 3 " MG Empl No 6	
"	22-12-16		No 2 commenced flying traverses	1 Lt Menieuts found unit
"	28-12-16		do do	
"	30-12-16		do do	
"	31-12-16		do No 1 Section relieved No 2.	R.E.

Commanding 62nd (Field) Co. R.E.

Vol 17
C/2nd Field Coy R.E.

WAR DIARY
or
INTELLIGENCE SUMMARY.

Army Form C. 2118.

Place	Date	Hour	Summary of Events and Information	Remarks and references to Appendices
In the Field	1-1-17	8am	No 1 Section working on dugouts GIRL ST, G11, & trench tramway	
			No 2 " " at WARLUS & surrounding villages, building bunking etc.	
			No 3 " " on dugouts, Stokes gun No 8, G520, Tunnel G18, 2" T.M Emplt.	
			No 4 " " dugout, Little GEM ST, dugout B3.B, making dugout frames	
			" " making & fixing steps for fire bays	
	3-1-17	"	No 1 — ditto	
			No 2 "	
			No 3 "	
			No 4 " " Repairs to dugout Battn H.Q. drainage Sucker Road & repairing tramway tracks.	
	5-1-17	"	No1 working with Special R.E. Remainder of Sections ditto as above.	Camouflage officer attached
	6-1-17	"	Work hampered by operations.	
	8-1-17	"	Working in "G" Sector dugouts etc	
	9-1-17	"	" " " Repairs to pump AGNY Lake No1 making sumps	
	11-1-17		" " " holes in trench tramway	Camouflage officer finished

Army Form C. 2118.

WAR DIARY
or
INTELLIGENCE SUMMARY.
(Erase heading not required.)

Instructions regarding War Diaries and Intelligence Summaries are contained in F. S. Regs., Part II. and the Staff Manual respectively. Title pages will be prepared in manuscript.

62nd Field Coy R.E.

Place	Date	Hour	Summary of Events and Information	Remarks and references to Appendices
La Fo Jute	13/7		No 1. Tramway widening trench, laying duck walk. Other sections as before.	
	15/7		do	
	16/7		No 1 attached to 61st Field Co R.E.	
	19/7		do	
	20/7		do	No 1 started dressing station GOWER ST. "trench strong, some from Toll Coy"
	22/7		do	
	23/7		No 1 not reported	
	24/7		No 1 men looking, talking, work as usual in afternoon	
	25/7		No 1 Sect. dugouts Sunken Road, No 2 Sec. dugouts, tramway & O.P's, No 4, dugouts, drainage, etc.	
	28/7		do	
	31/7		Work as before.	

Jno Malley Capt. R.E.
Commanding 62nd (Field) Co. R.E.

WAR DIARY
or
INTELLIGENCE SUMMARY.
Army Form C. 2118.

62 2nd Coy R.E.

62nd Field Coy RE

Vol 1. 8

Place	Date	Hour	Summary of Events and Information	Remarks and references to Appendices
In the Field	1-2-17	6pm	No1 Section on dugout in Sunken Rd. training etc.	
"			No 4 " working The Corps Arty positions, dugouts, drainage. SUNKEN ROAD.	
"	2-2-17	8am	No 4 " on dugout Sun St. Bomb St. GS4. Artillery positions for the Corps	
"			No 1 " " DAINVILLE & O.P. GEM ST.	
"			No 2 " " Sinking site at MARLUS	
"			" 3 " " OPs CORPS LINE (4).	
"			Work for all sections about similar to Frost.	
"	3-2-17	"	Nos 2, 3 & 4 as above. No 1 moved to DAINVILLE, for work on The Corps A.A positions	
"	4-2-17	"	Nos 2 & 3 " No 4 same as before, started dugout in Rly cutting	
"			No 1 Section working on dugouts in DAINVILLE gun positions, & OP Corps Line	
"	4-2-17	"	Sections " as before. Coy moved to ARRAS - BOULEVARD - DE - CARNOT	
"	9-2-17	"	Nos 1, 3 & 4 " " No 2 Artillery positions & O.P. RONVILLE, constructed with Rly plates & concreted.	
"	11-2-17	"	— do — do — No 4 started on OP. AGNY	
"	13-2-17	"	— do — do — No 4 commenced new dugout Rly bridge AGNY	17 Febry - sick to hospital 12 ??
"	17-2-17		Sections working as above.	

Army Form C. 2118.

WAR DIARY
or
INTELLIGENCE SUMMARY.
(Erase heading not required.)

62nd Field Coy. R.E.

Place	Date	Hour	Summary of Events and Information	Remarks and references to Appendices
In the Field	18/7	7am	No 1 working on dugouts (Rly DAINVILLE)(ARRAS RD), gun position (ARRAS RD) & OP (DAINVILLE)	
			No 2 " " Arty. positions Corps L.A. OP (PONVILLE) & OP (MAISON BRULEE)	
			No 3 " " & 60 pdr position G.32.d.9.8. No 4 Arty positions, dugout	
			Rly embkt. & OP's AGNY	
	20/7		Same as before	
	21/7		" " No 2 commenced OP BUCQUOY RD, No 4 commenced dugout GOWER ST.	2/Lt Taylor accidentally injured
	23/7			
	25/7		Sections working as above.	Lieut Lovell R.E. joined unit
	27/7		" " " Arty. positions, dugouts, OP's etc.	
	28/7		" " " "	

Major R.E.
Commanding 62nd (Field) Co. R.E.

WAR DIARY
or
INTELLIGENCE SUMMARY

Army Form C. 2118.

62nd Field Coy. R.E.

Nov/19

Place	Date	Hour	Summary of Events and Information	Remarks and references to Appendices
In the Field	1/3/17	8am	No 1 Sections at Dainville on gun positions, dugouts etc.	
	"	"	No 2 " , Arras, loops " , O.Ps for H.A.	
	"	"	No 3 " " " " dugouts	
	"	"	No 4 " " " " OPs at Agny, Grey St. & Rly. & dugout at Achicourt	
	8/3/17	"	Sections as before	
	16/3/17	"	do —— do —— do ——	
	19/3/17	"	Work stopped. Sections had orders to concentrate at billets owing to German retirement	
	20/3/17	"	Standing to. No 1 Sec. moved to ARRAS. Nos 3 & 4 Sec. digging tank crew Monument	
	21/3/17	"	No 2 Sec. salving R.E. material. Nos 1,3,4 Sec. on Dust dump RONVILLE	Lieut Lorenz wounded. First of several 22/3/17
	24/3/17	"	Nos 1 & 4 on Dust dump, No 2 Ammy fatls. Battery positions, salving material	
	"	"	No 3 Sec. on Ammy fatls & OPs for 12" H RGA.	
	25/3/17	"	No 2 As before. No 1, Tramway. BUCQUOY RD. No 4. Salving Tramway BUCQUOY RD.	" Capt King killed & 4 Sappers wounded
	27/3/17	"	As before. No 1 & 4 on new tramway	
	28/3/17	"	No 1 clearing BEAURAINS RD. 2-3 & 4 as before. No. 0 on Water Supply. Citadel ARRAS	Lieut Halley wounded
	30/3/17	"	As before.	Cpl Kane killed

Major R.E.
Commanding 62nd (Field) Co. R.E.

WAR DIARY
or
INTELLIGENCE SUMMARY.
(Erase heading not required.)

Army Form C. 2118.

Vol 20
(2nd Field Coy R.E.)

Place	Date	Hour	Summary of Events and Information	Remarks and references to Appendices
In the Field	1/7/17	6pm	No.1 Section clearing BEAURAINS Rd, erecting hut for 39th H.A.G., No 2 Sect working for 47th Bde R.F.A. No. filling gas cylinders, strengthening dugouts, ammn dumps etc for 26th & 47th Bdes R.F.A. No. 3 Sect ammn. fails etc. No. 4 on new tramway to BEAURAINS	
	4/7		2 about. No. 4 Sect making approach to South at CITADELLE ARRAS. Company moved to DAINVILLE.	115th Tunnel Co 10.3 115th Bourne No 7 joined unit
	6/7		No.1 Sect. Strengthening smaps SUNKEN ROAD. No. 2 loading bridges for R.F.A. No. 3 Sect. dugout for O.P. No. 4 Sect. making Brit. A.Q. CHRISTCHURCH CAVES RONVILLE.	
	8/7		Nos 2,3 + 4 Sections moved to BLANGY Rd Nr Groupe de Maisons in readiness for offensive. No 1 Sect took over R.E. Park DAINVILLE	
	9/7 10/7		Nos 2,3 + 4 Sections bridging trenches for advance of 26th Bde & 232 Bde to M.12 (S.A.) 51 S.H. No 3 Sect. Clearing road in NEUVILLE VITESSE to enable 12th Bde R.F.A. to move forward to M.13.	
	11/7		No 2 Sect. erecting water troughs on BEAURAINS-MERCATEL Rd. No 4 Sec. bridging trenches for 47th Bde R.F.A. to advance to M.13.	
	12/7 13/7	10.15am	Sections returned to Company A.Q. DAINVILLE. Company less No.1 section, moved to HABARCQ arriving 1pm (All map ref. Sheet 51.5.N.W.)	2 Bryside joined unit

WAR DIARY
or
INTELLIGENCE SUMMARY

Army Form C. 2118.

Place	Date	Hour	Summary of Events and Information	Remarks and references to Appendices
In the Field	14/7/17	5.30pm	Company less No. 1 Sec. moved to LIENCOURT arriving 12 noon	Lieut Sargent joined unit
	16 "		" Training, drilling etc.	
	21 "		" " "	
	22/7/17	11am	" musketry etc.	
	23/7/17	7am	" moved to BARLY	
	25/7/17	4.30pm	" " BEAUMETZ	
	26/7/17		" " N.20.b.6.8. NEUVILLE-VITESSE-MERCOURT road	
	27/7/17		No. 4 Sec. unloading pontoons & loading up wiring stores & Z.Crs. wiring support line in N.24.b	
	28/7/17		No. 2 Sec. relieved No. 1 Sec. at R.E. Park DAINVILLE. No. 4 Sec. digging shels for storing bombs N.23.d. No. 3 Sec. making R.E. dump at N.24.c.	
	29/7/17		No. 1 constructing 2 and foots N.24.c No. 4 Sec. digging communication trenches and repairing dugouts N.24.c. No. 3 Sec. making dump N.24 spare to dugout	
	30/7/17		No. 3 Sec. completed dump. No. 1 constructing and foots No. 2 laying out & supervising digging of C. trenches & assembly trenches.	

(All Maps ref. Sheet 51.b.5M)

signed. Major O.C.
Commanding 62nd (Field) Co. R.E.

WAR DIARY
or
INTELLIGENCE SUMMARY.
(Erase heading not required.)

Army Form C. 2118.

Vol N 2 / 62nd Field Coy RE

Place	Date	Hour	Summary of Events and Information	Remarks and references to Appendices
In the Field	1/5/17	7 am	N°1 Sect. constructing shelters E. of COJEUL. N°.2 Sec. at RE Park DAINVILLE. N°.2 on	
	2/5/17		N°.3 " " " N°.4 excavating for shelters	
	3/5/17		N°.1 Sect. N.23.D 85.40 splinter proof shelter. N°.3 splinter proof shelter N.23.d.65.25. N°.4 Sect. ditto N.23.D 55.20	
	6/5/17		N°.1.2.3.+4 Sects as before	
	8/5/17		N°.4 " " No.3 cutting down trees	
	10/5/17		N°.2.3 reloading " N°.1 splinter proof shelter N.23.D.S.2.	
	11/5/17		N°.1 & 3 Sect. erecting bow wire entanglement in front of EGRET trench N°.4 in billets.	
	13/5/17		No 1 " " & wiring EGRET trench. N°.3 Sect relieved N°.2 Sect at RE Park DAINVILLE. N°.1.	
	14/5/17		N°.1 & 2 wiring EGRET from Railway at O.19.c.7.7. to O.25.c.0.7. N°.4 camp work	
	15/5/17		3pes 1,2,+4 Sects working in camp owing to Relief.	
	16/5/17		N°.1 moving into 12W H.Q. No 2 & no work owing to operations	
	17/5/17		" 2+4 wiring in front of EGRET	

Army Form C. 2118.

WAR DIARY
or
INTELLIGENCE SUMMARY.
(Erase heading not required.)

_____ Field Company R.E.

Place	Date	Hour	Summary of Events and Information	Remarks and references to Appendices
In the Field	19/5/17	8am	Nos 1 & 2 wiring EGRET. No 4 out H.Q.	
"	20/5/17		No 1 Salvage.	
"	21/5/17		No 1 wiring EGRET. No 4 "	
"	23/5/17		Nos 1 & 3 Sec.ns wiring PANTHER. No 2 Salvage.	
"	24/5/17		No 4 " " "	
"	25/5/17		No 2 working in camp	
"			Nos 1, 2, 3 " MALLARD trench, No 4 digging EGRET trench about M30 a 9.5	
"	27/5/17		" 2, 3, 4 " "	
"			and crossing station at R.E. Bn. H.Q.	
"	28/5/17		Nos 1 & 2 continuing wiring PANTHER, No 4 into GOJEUL onto Rest scores	
"			ADS in CURLEW.	
"			No 3 deepening & widening EGRET, & crossing station at R.E. Bn. H.Q., widening	
"			track, & 2/5 at forward dumps.	
"	29/5/17		No 1 wiring along bank of GOJEUL from PANTHER to No 2 deepening	
"			EGRET and crossing station in CURLEW. No 4 crossing Br. in R.B.H.Q	
"			No 3 Salvage.	
"	31/5/17		Nos 1, 2, 3 standing to, No 2 laying duckboards in FOSTER Alexand, Valentine THE NEST & ALBATROSS	

Army Form C. 2118.

WAR DIARY
or
INTELLIGENCE SUMMARY.
(Erase heading not required.)

Instructions regarding War Diaries and Intelligence Summaries are contained in F. S. Regs., Part II. and the Staff Manual respectively. Title pages will be prepared in manuscript.

Place	Date	Hour	Summary of Events and Information	Remarks and references to Appendices
	31/1	Contd	Nº 4 crossing sh. at Right Bn. H.Q.	

E. Wempen Major R.E.
Commanding 62nd (Field) Co. R.E.

CONFIDENTIAL.

14th Division "A".

Herewith War Diary of 62nd Fd. Co. R.E. for the month of June.

Lieut-Colonel. R.E.
C.R.E. 14th Division.

4.7.17.

WAR DIARY
or
INTELLIGENCE SUMMARY.

(Erase heading not required.)

Army Form C. 2118.

Vol 22

Place	Date	Hour	Summary of Events and Information	Remarks and references to Appendices
In the Field	1/1/17	8 am	No 1 Sec. using COJEUL VALLEY. No 2 sec. excavating for ADS in CUTLEW trench & deepening EGRET trench	
	2/1/17	"	No 3 " " EGRET & making knife rests, camp work etc. No 4 Camp work & ADS in B.G² NQ	
	3/1/17	—	—	
	4/1/17	"	Company moved from N20.b.6.8 (2.5/6) to TELEGRAPH HILL BEARINS. No 4 Sec to DAINVILLE 3 OR wounded	
	5/1/17	"	" " TELEGRAPH HILL to M24.a.5.2.	
	6/1/17	"	No 1 Sect. hutting for ORG 14th Div. No 2 sec. advanced aid post in bunker road, using C1 & C2. No 3 Sect. erecting Aissances latrines etc. No 4 Sect at DAINVILLE workshops	
	8/1/17	—	by Major No 3 Section fur steps dpm bays C1, C2, C9 C3. No 1. A. "	Lt Edmonds
	9/1/17	4.30 am	4s. Sec. reconnoitre & Company moved to MONCHIET arriving 8.30 a.m.	joined Co.
	10/1/17	5 am	" " GAUDIEMPRÉ " 8.30 a.m.	
	11/1/17	4.30 am	" " PUCHEVILLERS " 8 a.m.	
	12/1/17	8 am	Training, physical drill, rifle drill etc. making targets for infantry	
	18/1/17	"	" " "	
	22/1/17	"	Company less 2 O & mounted section moved to ORVILLE for pontooning etc	Lt Gibbs posted
	24/1/17	"	" at ORVILLE, hutting	1620 Pioneer Pte 164/1
	25/1/17	"	" rejoined 2.O at PUCHEVILLERS.	

Army Form C. 2118.

WAR DIARY
or
INTELLIGENCE SUMMARY.
(Erase heading not required.)

6 Road Field Co. R.E.

Place	Date	Hour	Summary of Events and Information	Remarks and references to Appendices
In the Field	26/4	4p	Company resting.	
"	28/4	5.15a	Left PICHEVILLERS, & entrained at SAULTY-LARBRET 6p.m.	
	29/4		Arrival BAILEUL station 5.30am. Company marched to BLAKE CAMP M.28.c.3.3.	
	30/4	6p	Company moved to R.E FARM N.15.c.0.5.	

R.E.
Commanding 62nd (Field) Co. R.E.

WAR DIARY
or
INTELLIGENCE SUMMARY.
(Erase heading not required.)

Army Form C. 2118.

62nd Field Co. R.E.

Vol 23

Place	Date	Hour	Summary of Events and Information	Remarks and references to Appendices
L.N. 22	1/7		Coy. preparing camp at R.E. Farm N15.c.0.5.	
	2/7		" started work on Corps line. Wyschaete ridge defences. revetting trenches	
	4/7		" drawing wire for Strong points	
	9/7		" " " " " "	
	11/7		" " " " " "	Lt party of 180 O.R.s
				" " 129 "
	13/7		Secs. No 1 & 2 working on Corps Line. No 3 Sec. revetting. No 4 Sec. attd	Lt Rushall J (wounded B.)
	15/7		" No 4 Sec. wiring Corps Line	Lt Piggott J 1/7
				1 O.R. wounded
	17/7		" as before 127 S/pts attd	
	22/7		" " " 243 Camp work 100 Infy attd	
	26/7		" No 1,2,3rd revetting etc 139 " "	19th Frn wounded
			" As before 138 " "	2 O.R. killed 19/7
	28/7		" " " 155 " "	5 O.R. wounded
	30/7		Working on Corps Line as before	1 O.R. wounded
	31/7		Work stopped. Company resting - Inf reported unit 30/7	1 O.R. wounded
			Company standing to.	

Commanding 62nd (Field) Co. R.E.
Major R.E.

WAR DIARY or INTELLIGENCE SUMMARY

Army Form C. 2118.

62nd Field Coy R.E. Vol - 24

Place	Date	Hour	Summary of Events and Information	Remarks and references to Appendices
E.	1/7		Company at RE Farm N15.c.0.5. Standing to, drilling etc.	
the	2/7		" " " "	
Field	3/7		No 4 Sect re-commenced work on Corps Line defences	
	6/7	10:30a	Company moved to 27.V.5.c.4.3	
	11/7		" training, drilling, musketry etc	
	15/7	3pm	" moved to 28 G 27 b 5.8	
	16/7		" resting	
	17/7	2.30p	" moved to 28 H 30 a R.E. Transport to 28 H 33.a.5.2	
	18/7		" preparing camp, bivouacs	
	19/7		All Sections working on duckboard walk. HOOGE to GLENCORSE WOOD	3 O.R. wounded
	20/7		" 2x3 " " dressing station opp. ECOLE on MENIN RD, in HOOGE crater	
	21/7		" " " " 1.4 on duckboard track	
	26/7		" 2.3.4 " " " (Menin Rd.) 28 I 19.a.25.64	1 O.R. wounded 23/7
	26/7		Company resting	
	27/7		" moved to OTTAWA CAMP 28 G 24.c.5.4	1 O.R. wounded
	29/7		" " 27 X 10 b 5.9.	

[signatures]

WAR DIARY
or
INTELLIGENCE SUMMARY.
(Erase heading not required.)

Army Form C. 2118.

62 ZM Coy R.E.
Vol 25

Place	Date	Hour	Summary of Events and Information	Remarks and references to Appendices
L.R.Rd.	1/7	2.30p	Company moved from 27.K.10.b.5.9 to 28.T.16.b.2.9.	
	2/7		preparing camp.	
	3/7	8am	Sections working on NEW CROSS AVENUE trench, repairing, draining & revetting, FANNY'S C.T. revetting, trench boarding etc.	
	6/7		do. above. RESERVE LINE, new trench dug.	10R wounded
	6/7		NEW CROSS AVENUE, draining, revetting etc, FANNY'S C.T., digging trenches, SUPPORT LINE, revetting, clearing.	
	8/7		Work as before. R.A.P. Rt Bn. deepening trench, excavating. R. Bair H.Q. started as before. Excavation for R.A.P. completed. Rt Bn H.Q. handed over to 89th Fd Co RE	
	10/7		" " "	
	15/7		" " " Company H.Q. moved from 28.T.16.b.2.9. to 25.T.4.c.4.0	
	15/7			3 OR killed
	18/7			3 OR wounded
	21/7		Work on FANNY'S C.T., NEW CROSS, RESERVE LINE and GAPAARD GANGWAY repairing, draining revetting etc.	
	28/7		above work handed over to 89th Fd Co R.E.	

7

Army Form C. 2118.

WAR DIARY
or
INTELLIGENCE SUMMARY.
(Erase heading not required.)

Place	Date	Hour	Summary of Events and Information	Remarks and references to Appendices
Field	26/4		Wk as follows taken over from 89th 2nd Co RE. 3 O.Ps, Mule Track, Rt.Bn.HQ, Corps Line.	1 Officer wounded 29.4.17
	30/4		Wk as above.	

for Col Malley Capt RE.
Commanding 69rd (Field) Co. R.E.

Army Form C. 2118.

WAR DIARY
INTELLIGENCE SUMMARY.

(Erase heading not required.)

62nd Field Coy. R.E.
1.X.17 to 31.X.17

Vol 26

Instructions regarding War Diaries and Intelligence Summaries are contained in F.S. Regs., Part II and the Staff Manual respectively. Title pages will be prepared in manuscript.

Place	Date	Hour	Summary of Events and Information	Remarks and references to Appendices
In the Field	1/10/17 to 2/10/17		Company at 28 T 4 c.4.0. No 1 Section with 50 gunners (T.M.B) working on OPs of FANNY'S AV. No 2 Section with 100 infantry on mule track: No 3 on R.F. Bat'n H.Q. No 4 with 50 gunners (T.M.B) on Corps Defence Line	
"	5.10.17		Company standing by to move	
"	6.10.17	1.30 p.m.	Company moved to ASCOT CAMP, WESTOUTRE 28 M 8 d 10.2. T/2"Lt A.J.TOWLSON R.E. joined company	
"	7.10.17	9.30 a.m.	Company moved to 28 H 34 c. 3.7	
"	8.10.17		Company working on plank roadway PLUMERS DRIVE SOUTH	
"	9.10.17		Work in camp. No 1 & 2 Sections moved to advanced billets at 28 I 19 c.6.1.	
"	10.10.17		Company working on PLUMERS DRIVE SOUTH	
"	11.10.17 to 13.10.17		No 1 & 2 Sections working at A.D.S. at ECOLE 28 I 9 c.5.2 making road & buster to roof of cellars.	
"	"		Nos. 3 & 4 Sections working at Div. H.Q. erecting huts &c.	
"	13.10.17		Lt (a/Major) G.D.A. FENWICK R.E. left company. Capt. A.W.S. GIBSON R.E. arrived and took over command.	
"	14.10.17		No 2 Section working on road of ECOLE A.D.S. No' 3 & 4 Sect. work at Div. H.Q. No 1 Sect. returned to Coy. H.Q.	
"	15.10.17 to 17.10.17		No 2 Section working on road of ECOLE A.D.S. Nos 1 & 3 & 4 Sections work at Div. H.Q.	
"	18.10.17		No 2 Section —— ditto —— No 1 Sect. working at RIDGEWOOD CAMP (28 N 5 a). No 3 & 4 at Div. H.Q.	1 O.R. wounded (aeroplane bomb)
"	19.10.17 to 21.10.17		No 2 Section —— ditto —— Nos 1 & 2 Sect. working at RIDGEWOOD CAMP (latrines, cookhouses &c)	
"			No 4 Section work at Div. H.Q. T/Lt. E. EDMONDS R.E. to Base for dental treatment 20.10.17	

A.D.S.S./Forms/C. 2118.

Army Form C. 2118.

WAR DIARY
or
INTELLIGENCE SUMMARY
(Erase heading not required)

Instructions regarding War Diaries and Intelligence Summaries are contained in F. S. Regs., Part II. and the Staff Manual respectively. Title pages will be prepared in manuscript.

Place	Date	Hour	Summary of Events and Information	Remarks and references to Appendices
In the field	22.10.17		No 1 Sect Work at Ridgewood Camp, No 2 working on road at Ecole A.D.S, No 3 work in camp, No 4 work at Div H.Q.	
"	23.10.17		Nos 1, 3 & 4 Sections. Drill, Gas drill & work in camp. No 2 work on road at Ecole A.D.S.	
"	24.10.17		Nos 1, 3 & 4 Sections as above. No 2 Section returned to Coy. H.Q.	
"	25.10.17 to 26.10.17		Company working on fascine roadway from DORMY HOUSE (28 I 23 a 65) to junction of PLUMERS DRIVE SOUTH and JACKDAW SWITCH. Orders received from C.R.E. 9.30 p.m 26.10.17 to stand by to assist 89 F. Co. if required, in repair of PLUMERS DRIVE SOUTH & JACKDAW SWITCH which were reported damaged by shell fire and impassable for guns	
"	27.10.17		Request for help received from 89 F. Co. 2.20 a.m. Company went up and repaired roads.	
"	28.10.17		Company working on fascine roadway from DORMY HOUSE	
"	29.10.17		3 & 4 Sect. ditto. 1 & 2 Sections assisting 61st F. Co to complete junction of PLUMERS DRIVE WITH MENIN ROAD.	
"	30.10.17		1 and 2 Sections working on fascine roadway. 3 & 4 Sections standing by to assist 89 F. Co. with road repairs if required	
"	31.10.17		Company working on fascine roadway.	

[signature] Major R.E.
O.C. 62nd Field Co R.E.
31.x.17

Army Form C. 2118.

62nd Field Coy. R.E.
1.XI.17 to 30.XI.17
Vol 27

WAR DIARY
or
INTELLIGENCE SUMMARY
(Erase heading not required.)

Instructions regarding War Diaries and Intelligence Summaries are contained in F.S. Regs., Part II. and the Staff Manual respectively. Title Pages will be prepared in manuscript.

Place	Date	Hour	Summary of Events and Information	Remarks and references to Appendices
DICKEBUSCH	1.11.17		Company at 28 H 34 c. 37. No 1 & 3 Sections, Drill & work in camp. No 4 Section working on Fascine roadway from DORMY HOUSE (28 I 23 a 65) to junction of PLUMERS DRIVE SOUTH and JACKDAW SWITCH. O.C. met C.R.E. & Corps Troops and received instructions as to work to be done - hutting & stables. 1 O.R. wounded (shell)	
"	2.11.17		Nos 1, 3 & 4 Sections working for C.R.E. & Corps Troops. hutting & stables. No 2 Section on Fascine roadway	
"	3.11.17		Nos 1 & 4 Sections " " " " " " No 3	
"	4.11.17		No 2 Section resting	
"	"		Nos 2 & 4 Sections " " " " " " No 1	
"	5.11.17		No 3 Section resting	
"	6.11.17		Nos 2, 3 & 4 Sections " " " " " " No 1 section resting	
"	7.11.17		Nos 1, 2 & 3 Sections " " " " " " No 4 Section on Fascine roadway	
"	8.11.17		No 1, 3 & 4 Sections " " " " " " No 2 " " " "	
"	"		No 1, 2 & 3 Sections " " " " " " No 4 Section in camp	
"	9.11.17		Company loading wagons & preparing to move	
VLAMERTINGHE	10.11.17	10h	Company marched to VLAMERTINGHE. accommodated in huts at 28 H 9 a 4.0	
"	11.11.17		O.C. met O.C. 1st Canadian Field Coy. and went over work to be taken over & Plank road to SEINE (28 D 16 d 34.) No 3 Section with Transport marched to THIEUSMOEK	
"	12.11.17		Nos 1 & 4 Sections marched to POTIJZE exchanging billets with 2 Sections 1st Can F Coy at 28 I 3 d 8.1 No 3 Section by road and rail to HALLINES	
POTIJZE	13.11.17		HQ & No 2 Section marched to POTIJZE and into camp at 28 I 3 d 8.1. No 1 & 4 Sections working on Plank road to SEINE, doubling single road at I 14 b 95.55. No 3 Section billeted at HALLINES working under 42nd Inf. Bde	

Army Form C. 2118.

WAR DIARY
or
INTELLIGENCE SUMMARY

(Erase heading not required.)

Instructions regarding War Diaries and Intelligence Summaries are contained in F. S. Regs., Part II. and the Staff Manual respectively. Title Pages will be prepared in manuscript.

Place	Date	Hour	Summary of Events and Information	Remarks and references to Appendices
POTIJZE	14.11.17		Company working on plank road to SEINE. No 3 Section at HOLLINES working under 42nd Inf Bde.	
	15.11.17		" " " " No 3 Section marched to QUELMES	
	16.11.17 to 21.11.17		Company working on plank road to SEINE. Doubling and extending single road towards SEINE. No 3 Section at QUELMES - hutting &c and resting. 2 LIEUT W D STAVELEY R.E. joined unit 15.11.17	
	22.11.17		Company working on plank road to SEINE. No 3 Section rejoined company.	
	23.11.17		" " " " "	
	24.11.17		Company working on single plank road from 28 I 15 a. 0.7 Northwards.	
	25.11.17 to 28.11.17		Company working on plank road to SEINE. Extending single road to SEINE & maintenance from 28 I.15 b 35.25 forward.	
	27.11.17 28.11.17		Company working on plank road. Warning received that they would probably take over work of 490 Field Coy R.E.	
	29.11.17		No 3 Section only working on plank road to SEINE as working parties were cancelled at 7am.	
	29.11.17 to 30.11.17		Nos 1 2 & 4 Sections working on Plank Rd. until Infantry of 39th Divn If Cambridgeshires in 2 shafts. NOT det did not get on the job and 11th A bad day and it almost 9th Essex long time were shelled off. as they got there range guns were unusually Seem. to the Company House line coming in for a great deal active on "all back areas," boats gathering Some late in them. One driver slightly wounded. of attention and the "D"	

R.E. Fryer Capt Jr. R.E.
R.E.
o/c 62 Field Coy R.E.

Army Form C. 2118.

WAR DIARY
INTELLIGENCE SUMMARY

(Erase heading not required.)

62nd Field Coy. R.E.
1.12.17 to 31.12.17

Vol 28

Place	Date	Hour	Summary of Events and Information	Remarks and references to Appendices
POTIJZE	1.12.17		Company (less transport) at 28 I 3 d 8.1. Transport at 28 H 9 d 5.8. Company working on Timber road to SEINE 28 D 16 d 2.6 extending & maintaining road.	One O.R. wounded (Shell)
	2.12.17		No. 1 & 4 sections working on Northern Spur Plank road from 28 D 15 a 0.7. Maintenance. Remainder of Coy. preparing to move & taking over work from 490th Fd Co. R.E.	
YPRES CANAL BANK	3.12.17		H.Q. & 2.3.& 4 sections moved into billets on CANAL BANK at 28 C d 4.3. No 1 Section to VLAMERTINGHE. Transport to 28 H 29 1.6	
	4.12.17 to 26.12.17		Company working on construction of Corded Horse Standings and erection of Nissen Huts for R.F.A and 14th D.A.C. in YPRES and VLAMERTINGHE areas. Type of standings constructed:- Double. Each side 10' wide with 4' central feeding passage. Roofed with felt or corrugated iron. Standings of brick or concrete blocks.	
			No 4 Section to VLAMERTINGHE. 6.12.17	
	26.12.17 27.12.17	-	No: 1 & 4 Sections rejoined H.Q. at 28 C d 4.3. Transport moved to 28 H 9 d 5.8	
	to 30.12.17		Company working on Plank road from 28 D 14 b 85.65 to SEINE (28 16 d 2.6.) Maintenance and extension.	
	30.12.17		2 Lieut K.T. SPENCER R.E. (T.C.) joined Company.	
	31.12.17		Transport marched to ZERMEZEELE. Company preparing to move	

Dunglass
Major R.E.
O.C. 62nd Field Co. R.E.

WAR DIARY or INTELLIGENCE SUMMARY

Army Form C. 2118.

62nd Field Co. R.E.   1st Jan 1918 – 31st Jan 1918

Vol 29

Place	Date	Hour	Summary of Events and Information	Remarks and references to Appendices
YPRES	Jan 1st 1918	11am	Company marched from Canal Bank to Vaemertinghe Station entrained for Wizernes. Marched from here to St Martin au Laert (just N of St Omer). Transport marched from ZERMEZEELE via NOORDPEENE & CLAIRMARAIS.	
	2nd		Company at St Martin au Laert. Major Gibson to U.K. on Special leave.	Ill 28th to OK on leave
	3rd	6pm	Company entrained at 6pm at St Omer for EDGEHILL BURE–SUR–SOMME to join 5th Army	
	4th	8am	Arrived BURE 8am after intensely cold night. Coy detraining with side loading and no platform marched to EDGEHILL BURE–SUR–SOMME via DAVINCOURT – MEAULTE – BRAY – SUZANNE about 12 miles over very slippery roads causing many mishaps to transport. Arrived 4.15pm.	
	5th		Offloading wagons repairs to billets and general cleaning.	Sgt Savage 11am
	6th	9am	Company to Church Parade at CAPPY with 5th Ox & Bucks. No 1 Section to 5th Army Sniping School for work marching via BRAY – ALBERT – MILLENCOURT.	J.W. Lewis returned from lve
	7th		Drill, gas hut inspection and general cleaning. Very wet day.	
	8th		Drill, Musty and lashings and scheme for NCOs (budging) Very heavy snow all morning. No 3 Sectn work at CAPPY. Signalling school (PS)	
	9th		No 1 budging No 3 Demolitions and drill. No 2 AD for 6th at CAPPY	
	10 &		No 2 at CAPPY No 3 Budging No 1 Drill and demolitions	
	11th		No 3 at CAPPY No 1 Sec Musketry on range. No 3 lecture on demolitions Dumasts bridge	
	12th		No 1 Sec CAPPY No 2 Sec General clean up and fatigues No 3 Sec drill and range	
	13th	9am	Company to church parade at CAPPY with 5th Ox & Bucks. Beaten by 1st D.A.C. S.A.A. Sec at football 2–0. Coy transport after parade.	

WAR DIARY
or
INTELLIGENCE SUMMARY

(Erase heading not required.)

Army Form C. 2118.

Instructions regarding War Diaries and Intelligence Summaries are contained in F.S. Regs., Part II. and the Staff Manual respectively. Title Pages will be prepared in manuscript.

Place	Date	Hour	Summary of Events and Information	Remarks and references to Appendices
ECLUSIER	14th		No 1 Sec. work on Divn Sigs School CAPPY. No 2 & 3 Pontooning on Somme CANAL at CAPPY	at CAPPY
	15th		No 1 Sec finished work at CAPPY. Lt Browne i/c RE Course for 5th Oxon Bucks and 9th RBn	
			No 2 & 3 drill and chevalitons under Lt Shaughy. Lt Browne as for 14th	
	16th		Very wet day. Fitting R.E. lecture on bridging and gas drill in canteen. Bridge demantled	
	17th		Again very wet. Lecture on chevaltoma and knots and lashings in canteen. No 2 Sec beat mounted S.O.	
	18th		All Sections arms drill under C.S.M. Pontoon bridge across Somme Canal span 75ft. No 3 Sec beat No 1 Sec 3-2.	
	19th		Section drill all sections. No 2 on range. No 5/23 Guard duties and chevanking pontoon bridge. No 2 Sec beat No 3 Sec 5-1 in final.	
	20th		Company to Church Parade at CAPPY. All sections Pontoon rowing drill. No 4 section rejoined Cy. from 5th Army Sniping School. Major AWS Gibon rejoined from leave to U.K.	
	21st		Company washing wagons loading pontoons &c. 2nd Lt Tobitt rejoined from leave to U.K.	
			2nd Lt Lewis with billeting party to VRELY	
VRELY	22nd	9.0 a.m	Company marched to VRELY via CAPPY, PROYART, FRAMERVILLE, VAUVILLERS, ROSIERES with 42nd Bde Group. Arrived 3.0 p.m. and billeted for the night in empty houses. Good stabling for all horses	
BECQUIGNY	23rd	12.7 a.m	Company marched to BECQUIGNY via BOUCHOIR & GUERBIGNY arriving at 3.45 a.m. Billeted in empty houses. Stabling for all horses.	
"	24th		Orders received from 42nd Inf Bde cancelling previous orders to march to ECUVILLY. Company less transport remained at BECQUIGNY. At 11.15 a.m Transport marched to CANDOR (70 E - 3176) arriving after a 20 mile march at 9.0 p.m.	(70 E - 3176) 1:40,000

Army Form C. 2118.

WAR DIARY
or
INTELLIGENCE SUMMARY
(Erase heading not required.)

Instructions regarding War Diaries and Intelligence Summaries are contained in F.S. Regs., Part II and the Staff Manual respectively. Title Pages will be prepared in manuscript.

Place	Date	Hour	Summary of Events and Information	Remarks and references to Appendices
BEINES	25th	9.15 a.m.	Company (less Transport) marched to DAVENESCOURT and thence proceeded in Lorries to BERLANCOURT. From there marched to BEINES (66D.W.15.6). Transport arriving 5.30 p.m. BEINES arriving 5.15 A.m. Company billeted in empty hanger.	
"	26th		Company at BEINES. 2nd Lt. A.D. Lewis to BENAY to take over billets from French.	
BENAY	27th	9.50 a.m.	Company (less Transport) marched to R.E.Park. JUSSY. Arrived 12.30 A.m. Transport marched at 2 km and arrived JUSSY at 5 p.m. At 6.0 p.m. Company less transport and No 1 Sect. marched to BENAY (66S.H.21 central) being met by French guides at MONTESCOURT. Took over billets (good dugouts) from 5/57 Coy. French Engineers. 2nd Lt. Lewis went round line with French officers & took over stores &c. No 1 Section & Transport billeted in huts at R.E.Park JUSSY. Capt. R.E.FRYER. R.E in charge.	
"	28th		Nos 2, 3 & 4 Sections working in camp making latrines &c. No 1 at R.E.Park JUSSY. Organisation of Coy. for work is now as follows. H.Q. & 3 Sections at BENAY allotted to 42nd Inf. Bde. for work on line. One section at JUSSY in R.E. Workshops. Capt. FRYER appointed O/c Workshops. O.C. went round a line with B.M. 42nd Bde. A great deal of work to be done. No trenches revetted and fire trenches have no fire steps. Wire good and a number of good dugouts. Arranged with B.G.C. 42nd Inf. Bde. that company should work on the Main line of defence one section being allotted to each of the two batt? sector. The third section to be employed as required.	
"	29th		No. 2 & 4 Sections squaring up dumps at CAPONNE FARM. No. 3 Section constructing dugout for A.D.S at BENAY.	
"	30th		No. 3 Section constructing dugout for A.D.S of BENAY. No. 4 at Dump. No. 2 wiring with Amtry. from GHK R.E.C. 130 yds apron fence erected to close a gap which was found to exist in the wire of front line.	
"	31st		No. 2 & 4 Sections making brushwood hurdles. No. 3 working on A.D.S dugout.	

Langton M
Major R.E.
O.C. 62nd Fd. Coy. R.E.

WAR DIARY
INTELLIGENCE SUMMARY
(Erase heading not required.)

Army Form C. 2118.

62nd Field Coy. R.E.
1st Feb 1918 – 28th Feb 1918

Vol 30

Place	Date	Hour	Summary of Events and Information	Remarks and references to Appendices
BENAY	1st		H.Q. & 1,2,3 & 4 Sections at BENAY (66f H.21 central) No 1 Section & Transport at JUSSY.	
	2nd		Not joining personnel for Jessy Duval workshops. No 2 & 4 making hurdles in Infantry Road. No 4 on TRENCHES nothing.	
	3rd		No 2 revetting BRUCK. No 3 in Cmp dressing station OP.	
	4		No 3 making hurdles. No 3 & 2 do on 3rd Batt. Browne returned from leave to Bn.	
	5 & 6		do for 3rd. 2 Lt Toulson returned from a do for a do.	
	7		No 3 Corps HQ made a do for a do.	
	8		Rest — No 3 work in line. Also O.S.H. 2Lt Mills Coy take over work on Corps line from 3. Two men wounded and killed.	
	9		No 3 do for 2nd. No 4 OPs for Corps line (gunner). 2 Lt Fawcke to 5th Army Infantry School	
	10,11,12,13		No 2 and B4 work on strong point FOLLIS QUARRY and MT on OPs. No 3 on Mauberine [?] Battle Zone	
	14,15,6,17		No 2, 3, B4 working in front line and M.M. on OPs in Corps line.	
	18		Rest	
	19		No 2,3,B4 in front line MMs on OPs. Atkd Pioneer and 2 Sections work on gas screens for dress outs	
	20,21,22		No 2 & 4 working on Quarry Strong point No 5 in front line. Atk MMT in OPs. Atkd Infantry Coy No 3 Sect.	
	23		No 2 on Strong point No 3 in line MM on OPs. Gas screen party and Atkd Infantry Coy P 19	
	24, 25		No 3 new SP at Left Batt HQ. No 2 Wood SP at Quarry. MM on OPs. Inf working work No 3.	
	26, 27		No 3 do for sick. No 3 Sect on Battle Zone. Atk Infty on S.P. at Left Batt HQ. Major Green	
	28.		No 3 4 do for sick. No 2 Sect wire supervision of Coy did not work owing to the Gas party carried on with precautionary orders being received. Coy prepared to move at 15 min warning but later increased to 1hr warning.	

R.E. Major
a/6 62 Fld Coy R.E.

14th Divisional Engineers

62nd FIELD COMPANY R. E.

MARCH 1918

Attached:-

Report on Operations 23rd & 24th.

WAR DIARY or INTELLIGENCE SUMMARY

Army Form C. 2118.

62ND FIELD COMPANY, R.E.

Vol 31

Place	Date	Hour	Summary of Events and Information	Remarks and references to Appendices
BENAY MARCH	1, 2, 3		No 2 Started two dug outs in LAMBAY SWITCH working two shifts. No 3 BATTLE ZONE No 2 and attached Infantry started new work on ANGLETERRE Strong Point near URVILLIERS. Gas 300yds East of B47 Battery and Bde Hd Qrs at Les SAULES dug out.	
	4		No 2 working two shifts on dug outs in LAMBAY SWITCH with 7 O.R. of each shift by day and 40 carrying party by night. Dug out at LAMBAY FARM finished out. No 3 BATTLE ZONE 15/Nor N'hd E.R. attached O/R Parade on EVELYN Strong Point (late ANGLETERRE) and 1/5 No 4 unit Gas Screen party on dug outs in PERONNE TRENCH. O.C. 2 Bde. major sized EVA Strong Point (late VERDUN)	
	5		Do for Nº 4. Gas screen party finished dug outs in PERONNE TRENCH.	
	6		Do for Nº 5.	
	7		Nº 3 Sect Started Dug out in new position in MOROCCO Trench for machine gunners, other sections worked as usual. Gas screen party on dug outs in rearward zone.	
	8		Do for 7th Abnormal aeroplane activity on the part of E.A. probably due to exceptional day.	
	9		Sections as for 7th Summer time came into use.	
	10		Parade as for 8th Major A.D.B.R. Martin RE arrived to take over Command of the Coy vice Major A.V.S. Gibson RS evacuated to ENGLAND sick.	
	11		Nº 4 and attd Infantry worked on FUNNY Strong point the other two Sections as for 10th E.A. successfully driven off by Coy Lewis gun.	
	12, 13, 14		Do for 11th and A.J. Townson returned from leave to U.K. 12th.	
	15		2 x 3 Sects as before No 4 and attd Infantry working on dug out in Camb.	
	16		2 and 3 Sects on to for 15th Nº 4 Sect proceeded to SUSSY workshops to take over from Nº 7 Coy attd. J. worked on BATTLE ZONE	
	17		2 and 3 Sects and attd Infantry as for 16th Nº 7 Sect under 2Lt C. TOBITT marched to BENAY and took over Billets from Nº 4 Sect.	

WAR DIARY or INTELLIGENCE SUMMARY Continued

62nd Army FIELD COMPANY R.E.

Army Form C. 2118.

Place	Date	Hour	Summary of Events and Information	Remarks and references to Appendices
BERAY	18th		No 2 Sect on dug outs in LAMBAY SWITCH, No 3 Sect on BATTLE ZONE No 1 Sect and attacked Infantry worked on defended locality in the neighbourhood of LAMBAY from known as ELEGANT EMPIRE and ELSIE. Gas screen party working on dug outs in forward zone.	ELEGANT
"	19		as for 18 R.	
"	20		Nos 1, 2 & 3 sections + attn Field Infantry employed in completing six screens in which 9 42nd Bn Bde. Orders to take precautionary actions "issued" by WHAM 9 WAN M9. noted further + company ready to move at 15 minutes notice.	
"	21		Night of 20-21st passed quietly until 4:45am when enemy barrage of extreme intensity opened on all areas BERRY Village being one of enemy's main target. Word Action was received by runner from No 2 Bn Fd HQ about daybreak when orders were issued for No 2 & No 3 Sect to proceed to dug outs occupied by 15th Field Company at Les Sarres Ravine. No 2 Section proceeded in small party to CASTRES to report to C.R.E. C.S.M. WOODVER was mortally wounded and died later while running between No 2 Section Billet and Coy office with orders 2Lt CLARK with attd Ox & Bucks proceeded to Word Ride HQ with No 2 3 Sects No 1 Sect under Lt LEWIS prepared bridges for demolition in Jossy Aron. Jossy workshops were also very heavily shelled by the enemy with large calibre high velocity guns but Company were very lucky as only one man was slightly wounded. On arrival at CASTRES CRE gave orders to concentrate at Jossy at transport lines. About 2pm word had been received that the enemy had got possession of bridge to enable demolition to be carried out presence in front of bridge was leaving in No 2 Sect under O.C to proceed at once to DETROIT D'ANNOIS where it arrived in fact transport ordered by CRE to proceed at about 4pm No 2 3 Sects had orders to man a line of posts on the ridge.	

2449 Wt. W14957/Mg0 750,000 1/16 J.B.C. & A. Forms/C.2118/12

WAR DIARY or INTELLIGENCE SUMMARY

Army Form C. 2118.
62nd FIELD COMPANY, R.E.

(Continued)

Place	Date	Hour	Summary of Events and Information	Remarks and references to Appendices
BETHAY	21st		to the men of Bde Hq. The Huns held all day until at night orders were given to withdraw. O.C. slept at JUSSY on night. 2nd Lt. CARTWRIGHT No 2 Sec. killed on way down to CLASTRES from BERRY	
JUSSY DETROIT D'ARTONS	22		O.C. No 1 and No 3 Sects and No 1 Sect reported by at DETROIT in morning. No 1 Sect. had successfully destroyed all bridges under their charge after failed with the final experience reliable and cluttela. They entailed a great amount of extra work and some of the bridge were not destroyed until the enemy was on the opposite bank. At No 3 Railway bridge Sgt ARNOLD No 2 Sect performed a fine feat in wading into the water up to his neck under M.G. fire to fire a charge on a pile which was still holding up the main part of the bridge.	
LES RIEZ de CUGNY			About 1 pm while coy moved to an orchard at Les Riez de Cugny where the night was spent. Information had been received that the Germans in Nos 3, 5 & 7 Bks were not very far off. So orders were issued at 2 pm for a party to go up and attempt to enlarge the by means of Bangalore torpedoes. All Sect and 15 sappers No 1 Sec. left billet at 10 pm marched to FRAY but could find no B. Torpedoes so to SLABGC. On each bridge were led on planks and carried. It was impossible to intense F.M. Shell and M.G. fire to reach the business so party returned to Camp about 3.30 am. The night was light but after 11pm very misty. A party of the enemy about 150 strong were reported across the canal between Nos 1 & 2 bridges about 2 am and a great deal of shouting and firing was noticed. Statement 2nd Lt LEWIS reported Coy moved 5 am after 8 am. Tool Carts were halted in BEAUVIEU with sappers. Transport proceeded under	
LES RIEZ de CUGNY	23rd		Capt FRYER to GUIVRY via La NEUVILLE-EN-BEINE-UGNY-LE-GAY. They arrived at GUIVRY at 1 pm but at one received orders from CRE to proceed to MORAN COURT which was reached about 5 pm. Tool Carts	
MONTRALIMONT Fm BEAUMONT en BEINE			arrived also under instructions. Sappers dug in and prepared to light a detached post at MORAN COURT	
GUIVRY MORAN COURT	24th		of which is attached to this Diary. Transport billeted for night at MORAN COURT French gunners came in during night and opened heavy fire on HAM bridge head in morning with 3 14 gun batteries of 6" Hours. About 6 pm orders were received for transport to move at once.	

WAR DIARY or INTELLIGENCE SUMMARY

Army Form C. 2118.

62nd FIELD COMPANY, R.E.

Instructions regarding War Diaries and Intelligence Summaries are contained in F.S. Regs., Part II and the Staff Manual respectively. Title Pages will be prepared in manuscript.

(Erase heading not required.)

Place	Date	Hour	Summary of Events and Information	Remarks and references to Appendices
MUIRANCOURT	24th		to LASSIGNY which was reached about mid-night via BUSSY - SERMAIZE - LAGNY. Lt LEWIS killed by M.G. fire near VILLESELVE. 2/Lt KENYON also rejoined Coy.	
LASSIGNY RESSONS	25th		Transport moved at 5 a.m. to RESSONS via GURY - MAREUIL where it arrived about 11 a.m. and camped near the station. 2/Lt BROWNE with various Sappers rejoined the Company.	
RESSONS BRAISNES	26th		Company transport with various Sappers of all sections who had now rejoined (about 50) moved to BRAISNES via MARQUEGLISE	
BRAISNES MOYVILLERS	27th		Company moved about midday to MOYVILLERS via MONCHY - REMY - ESTREES - ST. DENIS where they arrived about 6 p.m. and had excellent billets vacated by the French.	
MOYVILLERS BEAUREPAIRE	28th		Company moved at 11 p.m. to BEAUREPAIRE via GRANDFRESNOY - PONT ST MAXENCE. A very unpleasant march owing to cold heavy rain, but Coy were lucky in getting ADRIAN huts for the night	
BEAUREPAIRE NOGENT	29th		Orders were received that Sappers would be entraining at NOGENT, transport proceeding separately. However late at night whole Coy was billetted at NOGENT the previous order being cancelled the march was via CREIL SUR L'OISE.	
NOGENT BAZINCOURT	30th		Coy marched to BAZINCOURT via CLERMONT. Another very wet march.	
BAZINCOURT FLECHY	31st		Coy marched to ~~MAIGNELAY~~ via ~~MAIGNELAY~~ - ~~MUIRANCOURT~~ VELLENES	

G. A. D. N. Martin
Major R.E.
OC 62nd Field Coy R.E.

Detailed Account of action of Company on
23rd & 24th March
1918

===================

At 8 a.m. on March 23rd, Sappers & Transport at CUGNY - LES - DIEZ received orders to move to BEAUMONT. On arrival there, with 61st & 89th Field Companies a position was taken up for one hour in the morning covering BEAUMONT to the West. Orders were received at 10.30 a.m. for the sappers to take up a flanking position on the line CUGNY - MONTALIMANT FARM & for the transport to move to GUIVRY. 2nd Lieut. Towlson R.E. was attached to C.R.E. as galloper. Sappers took up a position on the line ordered in a sunken road & remained there till 7 p.m.. Up to this time CUGNY was still in the possession of the British & the detachment of the King's Regt. were on the right of the position occupied by the Company, and other infantry were in front, but during the afternoon a flight of 12 German aeroplanes flew over the position occupied by the Company at 100' altitude machine-gunning the line but luckily causing no casualities. At 7 p.m. it was considered advisable to take up a more concentrated position round BEAUMONT, as a heavy German attack had captured CUGNY rendering the Company position open to enfilade fire. Positions round about & defending BEAUMONT were taken up by 62, 61 & 89 Field Coys., one Coy. of the King's Regt. & a detachment of Royal Irish Regiment. Col. O'Leary, R.I.R. being senior officer present, took command. The Company "stood to" all through the night and at 6.30 a.m. on the morning of the 24th an order was received (through Major Ormston R.E.) from Col. O'Leary for the Company to rejoin its transport which it was understood, was at GUISCARD. The Company marched down the road through VILLESELVE as far as BETHANCOURT when it was stopped by the G.O.C. 36th Division & ordered back to BEAUMONT (order attached). It therefore retraced its steps as far as VILLESELVE where its orders were again cancelled by G.O.C. 61st Bde. & it was ordered to take up its position in the sunken road running E. & W. at MONTALIMANT FARM. The Company took up their position alongside 89th Field Coy. R.E. an Army Troops Coy. R.E. & details of R.I.R., M.G.C. etc & found themselves being heavily shelled from the rear by our own guns (or the French) and also from in front by German H.E. & shrapnel shells. At about 2 p.m. troops were seen coming into a position to our rear (south) & the sun being in our eyes the troops were taken to be Germans who were supposed to have made their way round our flanks. It was decided to remain in our positions & face the German attack from front & rear but ten minutes later the details on the right of the position left their line to attack the Germans in rear, and so it was considered advisable to have concerted action & the whole line retired to attack the position of VILLESELVE. It was at this moment that Lieut. Lewis R.E. was killed by M.G. enfilading fire from the direction of CUGNY. During this retirement to attack, the Company passed over ground which was being heavily shelled by H.E. & shrapnel from the North, but no fire from VILLESELVE & when only some 150 yards from VILLESELVE it was recognised that the troops in VILLESELVE were

Contd :-

French and not German. By this time the large number of odd infantry details without officers or N.C.O's had returned to the attack of VILLESELVE disjointedly, so the Company under 2nd Lieut. Browne R.E. having moved toward BEAUMONT to try and enfilade VILLESELVE, turned & faced the enemy more or less on the line of the VILLESELVE - CUGNY road, the O.C. Coy. at the time being engaged in reforming the infantry details. After half an hour the retirement ceased and single man holes about VILLESELVE occupied, but only for the space of an hour when German troops were seen to be out-flanking the position, a further retirement was ordered(by whom it was not known)by ½ platoon from the right. Reinforcements had come up from the direction of BETHENCOURT & been pushed into the Southern & Eastern edge of VILLESELVE to try & hold up the German attack from this quarter,& this enabled the second retirement to be stopped & a fresh position to be taken up just North of BETHENCOURT - VILLESELVE road. Various local counter attacks were made with partial success at this turn by cavalry & infantry but at 4 p.m. a heavy concentration of smoke & shrapnel fire was brought on to the Southern end of VILLESELVE & the troops holding it retired. Efforts were made to reform these troops in extended order across the VILLESELVE - BETHENCOURT road but it was found these troops would not hold , owing to the strain of 4 days fighting, lack of officers,N.C.O's and the mixture of men from many units, so they were marched back through the French line to GUISCARD & BOURCHIES.

Major R.E.
Commanding 62nd Field Company R.E.

COPY of order received from G.O.C. 36th Divn. at BETHENCOURT at 8.50 a.m. on 24/3/18.

To.O.C. 62nd Field Company R.E. & 89th Field Company R.E.
No.T.C.17. dated 24.3.18
    You will return to the Line and take up a position on the right of the 1st R.I.R. from R.25.c.10.50 to R.31.a.80.75
                (Signed)
8.50 a.m.

       Certified true copy   *A.D.M. Martin*
                                  Major R.E.
            Commanding 62nd Field Coy.R.E.

COPY of order received at VILLESELVE from G.O.C. 61st Bde. at 10 a.m. on 24/3/18.

To O.C's 62nd & 89th Field Companies R.E.
    Your previous orders are cancelled & you are to take position facing North in road MORTALIMONT FARM – CUGNY
                (Signed) M.Cochrane B.G.
10 a.m.   Comdg. 61st Bde.
24.3.18

Certified true copy
A.D.M. Martin
Commanding 62nd Field Coy R.E., Major R.E.

14th Div.

WAR DIARY

62nd FIELD COMPANY, R.E.

APRIL

1918

WAR DIARY or INTELLIGENCE SUMMARY

Army Form C. 2118.

62 Fd Coy R.E.

APRIL 1918   Vol 32

Place	Date	Hour	Summary of Events and Information	Remarks and references to Appendices
	April 1918			
NEUILLES – FLECHY	1	8.45am	Coy marched at 8.45am to FLECHY via FROISSY – HARDIVILLERS – arriving about 4 pm.	
FLECHY – VERS	2	8.15am	Coy marched at 8.15am to VERS via BONNYEUX – les – EAUX – FLEURS-SUR-NOYE – ST BROCHEU – FLACHY – BUYON – BACOUEL	
VERS – AUBIGNY	3	11am	Coy marched at 11am to AUBIGNY via SALEUX – AMIENS – LONGEAU – GLISY – BLANGY-TRONVILLE forward hand-carts on GLISY-BLANGY Rd just beyond GLISY. Rear heavy transport on AMIENS – ST FUSCIEN Rd at 5 Cross roads	
"	4		Coy stood to all day and all night and manned trenches Sth of AUBIGNY on ridge	
"	5		Coy together with 1st and 89th Field Coys completed trenches on AUBIGNY line. Marched to BLANGY-TRONVILLE and billeted there arriving at 8pm	
BLANGY	6		Coy marched out and cover shelters to H3rd Bd HQ at 1 Kilo West of AUBIGNY	
"	7		Coy at work throughout day on improving road to pontoon bridge over SOMME River just to North of GLISY. Marched in evening with forward hand-cart to billets in South AMIENS	
"	8		Heavy transport marched at 12.20pm to FRESNOY – AU – VAL. Coy in billets at South AMIENS resting, bathing etc.	

WAR DIARY or INTELLIGENCE SUMMARY

Army Form C. 2118.

(Erase heading not required.)

Instructions regarding War Diaries and Intelligence Summaries are contained in F.S. Regs., Part II and the Staff Manual respectively. Title Pages will be prepared in manuscript.

Place	Date	Hour	Summary of Events and Information	Remarks and references to Appendices
AMIENS	9th		Coy remained at AMIENS. Heavy transport marched to FRUCOURT via MOLLIENS VIDAME le QUESNOY- AIRAINES and HALLENCOURT. Light transport marched to ALLERY	
MONCHAUX	10th		Coy entrained SALEUX at 7.45 pm arrived at GAMACHES 8 am morning of 11th and marched to MONCHAUX. Heavy and light transport marched to MONCHAUX via OISEMONT- RAMBURELLES TRANSLAY- GAMACHES.	
"	11th		Coy rested at MONCHAUX.	
CITERNE	12th		Coy marched at 2 pm to CITERNE via BIRMQY- RAMBURES - OISEMONT.	
FORET DE VIGNACOURT	13th		Coy marched to Fd FORET DE VIGNACOURT near FRINCOURT via ALLERY- ARAINES - LE QUESNOY - HANGEST BOURDON- FLIXECOURT. Camped in forest.	
"	14		Transport marched to CANDAS via SY OUEN - BOMART- EN- PONTHIEU- BERNEUIL- FIENVILLERS.	
ECOUEDECQUES	15		Coy entrained at 9 am and proceeded to ECOUEDECQUES arriving at 4.30 pm. Transport marched to HERLIN-LE-SEC via LONGUE VILLETTE - HEM - OCCOCHES - NEUVILLETTE - FRE VENT and NUNCQ about 22 miles	
"	16		Transport marched to ECOUEDECQUES	
"	17 to 30th		Whole Company employed in digging a defensive G.H.Q. line from about 0.35 Central through LE PIRE - V.I.C.1.2 - Village of CANTRAINNE - crosses the LA NAVE RIVER at V.T.b.8.4 - follow river to V.8.a.65 thence to boundary on road at V.8.d.0.8	

Place	Date	Hour	Summary of Events and Information	Remarks and references to Appendices
ECQUEDECQUES	17th - 30th April		The work also included the defence of the village of L'ECLEME. This starts at CHATEAU DE QUESNOY P.32.d.6.0. follows round in front of L'ECLEME and finishes at Bridge over LA NAVE RIVER at V.10.a.1.8. The position in orchards and other places strengthened by a series of groups of huts provided by Portuguese infantry. The labour of approximately 150 each. In addition to digging two rows of wire line was wired with a double apron fence.	
	2nd 17th		2/Lt Preston R.E. joined the Company from base. 2/Lt Thomas, Furlong, Broadway, R.E. and 28 Sappers joined the Coy for work on defences.	

R.E. Fryer Capt R.E.
for O.C. 62 Field Coy R.E.

WAR DIARY or INTELLIGENCE SUMMARY

Army Form C. 2118.

Vol 33 — May 1918

Place	Date	Hour	Summary of Events and Information	Remarks and references to Appendices

LECQUEDECQUES — May 1st

Sections and the attached sections working on L'ECLEME - CANTRAINNE - CHATEAU-du-QUESNOY positions the Labryn being provided by the Portuguese 28 Machine Gunners and the 9th & 95 & 10th 23rd Batt.ns Portuguese Infantry. The average strength of the P.I. was about 150 and the infantry about 200. We had no practically all cover in the building breastworks with 6 ft cover as the ground in this neighbourhood does not permit of a trench being dug to a much greater depth than 1 ft to 1 ft 6. All the beginning of the month the Coy worked with the Portuguese in two shifts but later on this method was altered to one shift of task work starting at 7 am. When on the 10th May the 35th Batt.n was used for work infantry letting than finding work. On the 13th the 35th Batt.n was used for Coy. Canadian Corps were tried on this job to cart worked with the Coy. and worked well in places but in many places the soil for baskets and for scooping without previous ploughing. The ground was too hard allowed to be destroyed how there were growing crops were not allowed to the great number of places these spots absolutely necessary they were not

O.S.M. Caw's joined the Company from Base Depot

10th See the 10th the 35th Batt.n P.I. were allotted to 1st W Field Company, for work on BUSNES SWITCH.

Army Form C. 2118.

WAR DIARY Cont'd MAY 1918
INTELLIGENCE SUMMARY
(Erase heading not required.)

General Bela Cont'd

Place	Date	Hour	Summary of Events and Information	Remarks and references to Appendices
EQUIECOURT	11.5		Major ? De R Davis was admitted to hospital through in + Lieut Aulahann went	
	15		Capt Harvey RS found the Company from 61st Field Coy as acting OC.	
			Lt Towson RS proceeded on 14 days special leave to UK for family reasons.	
Mercatel Arras	19th		Competition between the three posts of the Field Companies was held at Ham Pl.	
			At Ham the pictures were the GOC (Genl Skinner) Col Colvill Mr Col Richards RSC Col Herd Mr Dore RC	
			The Competition was very interesting and a practical turn out in every way.	
			So much so that the judges had difficulty in placing the winners. No 89 ?	
			Field Coy won with 890 points the Coy being 2nd with 887 and ? 881	
			Full Coy 3rd with 860. We water cart of the Coy got 1st prize ?	
			the Cook of the three.	
	20th		Nos 2 and 4 and RAF S/MS proceeded to billets and bivouacs at L'ECLEME	
			at V3.C.0.73 in after the Division move back	
	15		Capt Harvey RE and Cpl (A/Sgt) Cross mentioned in Dispatches London Gazette	
			dated 15th May 1918	
	22nd		I returned at morning Battle Stations was carried out in the evening	
			The training of tactics work with PORTUGESE troops on tactical offensive	

WAR DIARY
or
INTELLIGENCE SUMMARY.
(Erase heading not required.)

Army Form C. 2118.

2nd Field Co. R.E.

Place	Date	Hour	Summary of Events and Information	Remarks and references to Appendices
	27th		found on digging down that they had were to work 6 hours than to undertake work that took 1 great to [?] to their type so on an average after spending a task they seemed as if 6 hours allowing only about 20 cubic feet so it seems preferable to give a small task for the whole hour, they are cleverer in taking if nothing up and motivate out quickly & well. Sent one to be far advanced to the CANTRAINE DEFENCES & L'ECLEME that the line at BEAUREPAIRE (a new front line) was begun & excellent progress made. No wire in front but 2 or 3 days work would make the line fightable from the ENGRS	
	28th		CANTRAINE R.D. onwards to L'EPIRE. Artillery left C.S. a/a 62 etc etc b/y	

WR 34
62nd October
62nd October

WAR DIARY
INTELLIGENCE SUMMARY
June 1918

Army Form C. 2118.

Place	Date	Hour	Summary of Events and Information	Remarks and references to Appendices
FRUEDECQUES	JUNE		Work continued as in previous month on defensive works from CHATEAU DU QUESNOY, Northward to the canal at PONT LEVIS, with the 35th Pioneer bn, Bothm, 1st Portugese Sappers & Miners & 1 Section 1 R.E. At the end of the month the work of construction of belt of wire had completed wire fixed c. 1500 yds long each consisting of detached posts each of 2 aprons including farm P20 b 2.1. to P20 c 10.5. from b.26 a.9.1. to P26 b 2.1. & from P26 b 20.2. P26 D 6.5 in several places are filled in with barbed wire. The support line S of CHATEAU DU QUESNOY a broke on the NAVE switch (between a inclusive thence to the LECLERE Alleres) are worked on by the 24th Battalion P.I. Owing to the shallowness of Sylvange line 2 battalions defences from the 16th to the 23rd inclusive. The front line of Contrainne defences to the back at U 6 C 10.3 from the Southern Boundary at V 8 D 2.7 allotted to the 25th Bn Both'n, P.I. is about complete but part of these trenches are too narrow for firebays. The 13th Battalion late 2 days, 9 days have worked on the winner line of the CONTRAINNE defences, which is inclined completed from V14a 1.7 to V7 D 2.8. The Northern line I have from CATRAINNE RD to E5 P.I.E. and in through not jumping only except in 4 stitches which have a reverse fire slope, available. 30. 10/6/18 for Halley Hughes R.E 62nd Field Coy R.E

WAR DIARY
or
INTELLIGENCE SUMMARY.

Army Form C. 2118.

Ent: JUNE 1918

62 M Batt RE

Place	Date	Hour	Summary of Events and Information	Remarks and references to Appendices
EQUEDEQUES	24th		Worked with Infantry who withdrew 2/- on the Somme South	
			The forward positions billeted at L'ECLEME were relieved on the 24th after work & came back to H.Q.	
	23rd		62 Sports were held on Sunday the 23rd proving a great success. The men enjoyed them & all the events were very well completed. The day of was not interrupted by any news as no word came by the 24th, 25th but the men were The G line of Influenza till the 25th. On the 30th there were 30 men down with it. Its effect is to incapacitate a man for 2, 3 or 4 days leaving him rather weak	
			Jos Halley Major RE OC 62 nd Field Coy.	

62ND FIELD COMPANY, Army Form C. 2118.

WAR DIARY
INTELLIGENCE SUMMARY
(Erase heading not required.)

JULY 1918.

Place	Date	Hour	Summary of Events and Information	Remarks and references to Appendices
EQUEDECQUES	1st		Work proceeded on the LILLERS-STEENBECQUE LINE & the L'ECLEME- BUSNES LINE very satisfactorily till the 8th.	
CLAIRMARAIS FOREST	8th		On the 9th the Coy entrained for CLAIRMARAIS FOREST where it remained till the 12th when the Coy received orders to proceed to ST SYLVESTER	
ST SYLVESTER CAPPEL	12th		CAPPEL to form the Divisional work on the WINNIZEELE LINE. A reconnaissance of which I had made with Gen. GILLAM CE village Lt. Col. CLOSE CRE of the Div. & Major Templeby GSO1 of the Div. We accepted that the village which was commenced on the 16th inst. with 2 Coys of the 33rd London Regt. manning the front line, consisting the parapet. 3 Coys were provided the following day. 1 Coy of the 6th Welch 2 Coys of the 6th it will began work on the 18th. 1 Coy of the 1st North Lancs (Pioneers) on the 19th. 21 Toulsers reported from base on 19th	
	21st		Sunday no work but Coy paraded for Church and afterwards an hours Company drill.	
	22nd		N19 Sec and the Coy of Loyal North Lancs Pioneers started wiring the Picket Line of the WINNIZEELE line starting from the	

62ND FIELD COMPANY R.E.
Army Form C. 2118.

WAR DIARY
INTELLIGENCE SUMMARY.

Ref Sheet 27   July (contd)

Place	Date	Hour	Summary of Events and Information	Remarks and references to Appendices
ST SYLVESTRE CAPPEL			Head at Q.35.c.1.1. and working southwards until joining the West Cheshire Line. 2 Coys of 6th Wilts were working with N°2 S.S. 2 Coys each of 33rd London Regt (RB) with numbers N° 4 and 3 Sees all in the grass fields from P.36.C.3 q to P.36.C.7.O. They completed the left half of this and (he) up to 6ft Cover on the 26th. Some more Bill boxes were erected one by N°4 at P36.c 85.95 and another at P.30.c.7.4. An interesting job as the Coy had not previously erected any of these boxes the whole boards and brands marking to front line were erected during the week. Rain seriously interfered with the work on the 24th and 27th. The 25th was a glorious night with a full moon and quick air activity but no bombs fell near the camp.	
	29th		The 33rd London Regt were relieved by the 29th Durham L.I. 30 W.P. were got from either to-day.	
	31st		6th Wilts were relieved by 14th M.S.H. and An inter Company relief by the Pioneers so WP0 were seriously restricted to-day.	
	29th		OC went round with CRE OC Dvnd M.G. Battn and Corps MG	

WAR DIARY
or
INTELLIGENCE SUMMARY

(Erase heading not required.)

Army Form C. 2118.

62ND FIELD COMPANY. R.E.

Contd

Place	Date	Hour	Summary of Events and Information	Remarks and references to Appendices
	24th		officer and various M.G. emplacements were sighted. It was decided to put in M.G.R Pill boxes at V.6.a.7.8 one and two in bomb hole of P.36.b.9.9. Another Pill box was taken over from 98th Field Coy R.E. at P.11.C.3.3 and also a gunner OP in the Mill. The 89th Field Coy went out of the area on 31st July and everything was handed to 62nd Coy R.E. Various reinforcements have arrived during the month so the Coy is now only 9 men understrength.	
	29th		2nd Toulson was cross posted to 122nd Field Coy R.E. 36th Reinf and 2nd Mercier was ordered to join us but has not yet done so.	

R.E. Dryer Capt RE
a/oc 62nd Coy RE
31/7/18

WAR DIARY
or
INTELLIGENCE SUMMARY

(Erase heading not required.)

Army Form C. 2118.

AUGUST 1918   V.11. 36

62ND FIELD COMPANY R.E.

Place	Date	Hour	Summary of Events and Information	Remarks and references to Appendices
ST SYLVESTRE CAPPEL			Ref Sheet 27 S.E	
	1st		Coy working on the NINNEZEELE FRONT LINE from the main road at P.30.c.7.8 to our Southern boundary at V.6.c.2.0. The work consists of altering the existing trenches into a line of resistance, revetting firebays to give 6ft of cover throughout. The labour was provided by the 4th No S.W. and the 20th D.L.I turning out something like 300 men each for day. Besides work on the trenches the Coy have to put in 5 concrete Pill Boxes. Machine gun emplacements of Sir Ernest Moirs design.	
	5th		Bomen of Coy went in two lorries to the Divisional Horse show at EPERLECQUES which was a very great success.	
	8th		Work continued on the NINNEZEELE front line till the 12th.	
ST MOMELIN	12th		The Coy less transport entrained at STEENVOORDE for ST MOMELIN. Transport travelled by road & arrived same day.	
QUEST MONT (EPERLECQUES)	13th		Followed the move by road & coy to be located near WATTEN & then moved to the left. The Coy arrived at QUEST MONT till the 19th [illegible]	

WAR DIARY or INTELLIGENCE SUMMARY

Army Form C. 2118.

62ND FIELD COMPANY R.E.

Aug 1918

Place	Date	Hour	Summary of Events and Information	Remarks and references to Appendices
OUEST MONT EPERLECQUES	14th		The Buffets Sports still continuing till 12.30.	
			Went round & saw it. Fall over to [illegible] horse hurdle & he [illegible]	
			hitting a standing gas.	
	15th		The 6 schemes were tried at BLEUDECQUES as a [illegible] [illegible]	
			CCS.	
	16th		The 6th [illegible] [illegible] which [illegible] [illegible] [illegible] [illegible] know there are no [illegible]	
			that [illegible] [illegible] are [illegible] by the GOC to keep [illegible] at	
			EPERLECQUES & the are afterwards cleaned with the [illegible] [illegible]	
			[illegible] whilst [illegible] is the [illegible] than they have been employed.	
			A. & SOC came & walked around.	
	17th		A big trial of new [illegible] to CALAIS for the day.	
	18th		Arrived & [illegible] [illegible] in on the afternoon & checked by the heat that	
			we have before us here with the Division.	
LONGUES	19th		The Coy moved to LONGUES where [illegible] [illegible] [illegible] till the	
	22-23rd		[illegible] [illegible] the Coy moved up night. Platoons [illegible] [illegible] [illegible]	
			afternoon.	

WAR DIARY or INTELLIGENCE SUMMARY

Army Form C. 2118.

62ND FIELD COMPANY, R.E.

Aug 1918

Place	Date	Hour	Summary of Events and Information	Remarks and references to Appendices
LOUCHES	22nd		The transport left at 9 am on a 3 days trek to PROVEN under the command of Lt STUDLEY, the rest being all	
PROVEN	23rd		The Coy entrained at NORTBECQUE for PROVEN from which station they marched to DIRTY BUCKET CAMP to begin work under the 11 Corps. Transport arrived on the 24th. The work taken over was of constructing of 3 proposed shelters on the approach of GREEN LINE. A system of 21 men with a Serjeant-marked to each shelter. This work was begun on the 26th & contained up to the 27th	
YPRES	28th		The Coy moved to the Canal bank by Lorries clothing their practice work 100 x west of the WAIL END.	
	29th		Note a reconnaissance of the Trenches & began work on the RESERVE LINE with 2 Offs & N.C.O.s of N.Z. Engineers to 2 advanced	
	30th		this work was one being carried on by my self. The work was similar to that carried on by the Kiwis, NOD visiting my pleasant day with 1 Off of Infantry engaged in delivering shelter for R&E. a Batt" H.Q. at 28th H.S.C 12 & 11. 63 N.03	
	31st		Sulves another K Barr is reported for the Wambelge. a second three for Valley between P.O., at 62 infants by	

WAR DIARY or INTELLIGENCE SUMMARY

Army Form C. 2118.
62nd FIELD COMPANY R.E.
SEPTEMBER 1918
Vol 37

Place	Date	Hour	Summary of Events and Information	Remarks and references to Appendices
YPRES			KEMMEL. Pioneer labour on 30, 31st Aug, was held up awaiting a fresh supply of limpets & dingbats arriving same from the C.R.E. to advance charges from Dickebusch & there some were dismantled. The charges & their grids to be maintained E. of Ypres. In the meantime the platoons withdrew all the charges sent to BRANDHOEK DUMP. No. 3 Platoon have become available to work & were eld to reform the bridge across the Col. sluices at YPRES – COMINES CANAL from the YSER CANAL. No. 4 platoon continued work at Batn HQ 28th & 5 C.L.R. 2nd Batn HQ T16a63. No. 2 platoons at thirty. Two work consists of supplying Explod & Shellout after erecting another at 1 Batn HQ. & erecting 3 Shellouts (3 are completed by the above (6) 209.WH.W(?) at Battn HQ. No 1 Section carried on with their work E. of Ecole on nullity. O.P. to Ks were 4 shuft trenches & building Pillbox for part of the ECOLE. The Pillbox Shelter is made up of an elephant gun arched roof. 7 feet of concrete refs is employed.

62nd
FIELD COMPANY
R.E.

WAR DIARY
or
INTELLIGENCE SUMMARY. September 1918
(Erase heading not required.)

Army Form C. 2118.

Place	Date	Hour	Summary of Events and Information	Remarks and references to Appendices
YPRES			with 2 S/S. who were visited. Shell half filled.	
			No further touched their work.	
			Went over to the 1st the N. Lanes & carried	
			on work on a similar scale, completing 2 lift machine a	
	2nd		beginning work on another.	
				VERMONT at
DIRTY BUCKET AREA			We were relieved by the 90th Field Coy (98th Div) The Coy entrained at 5.30pm on the	
			light railway running to DIRTY BUCKET AREA about 6.	
	19th		The Coy arrived & changed trains in the evening receiving orders to be ready to move to	
DICKEBUSCH AREA	19th		take over billets of the 237th Field Coy Scottish to English Stables at HAGUE	
			FARM & the Forlen of OUDERDOM as soon as the MO to the Divn. The move was	
			taken by lorry to the site. We took over the new billets at A.26.c.19.	
			Put in charge of the Stables. Began work at night on new billets. The line	
	20th		No 1 Section was detached to build shelters many & up by Light railway to HAMEL Class	
			to CAFE BELGE. The railway was taken (?) Skelton & company to Siding arrived 6th Div.	
			following my NN-2F-8F-32 and NoR.2-3 Sections detached to build covering from BUCKMASTER	
			FARM to RIDGE WOOD. No 4 Section commenced construction of a trenchrail on the Rienn	
			from Lighthouse way from ENGLISH WOOD to VOORMEZEELE Switch. No Section to the	

WAR DIARY
INTELLIGENCE SUMMARY

Army Form C. 2118.
62ND FIELD COMPANY R.E.

SEPT 1918

Place	Date	Hour	Summary of Events and Information	Remarks and references to Appendices
DICKEBUSCH AREA			**VOORMEZEELE – ST. ELOI**	
	25/9		Work. Lt Brownrigg with No 5 Sectn worked on the 2 tracks of the ridge with material salved from the site. Remainder his section worked as infantry towards morning to relieve 2nd Stn on the site. Lt Twill carried on with No Westn in 48th Divn area, filling in shell hole & Stg billeting with No 2 Sectn. Meeting of Pioneers & No Sectn carried on with the job today. There was considerable shelling but no casualties. Enemy shelling on the O.B.S. and the Shelly.	
	26/9		was going very heavy. Communication trailway to Scotch Farm being pushed on. The line was laid immediately behind going. Also A road was completed. Enemy shelling was also very heavy throughout the day & night. Sports Coy complete.	
	27/9		The work Lock & RIDGE Road was carried on to 4th Division when Lt Twill's sectn came to VOORMEZEELE – ST ELOI Rd from T.31.d.2.6. L.R.V.S. from the 50th Lt Brownrigg's sectn with No 2 Sectn of 12th E.R.H.E.s worked on making the approaches at the other end of the road leading to MOND-DAIT. Stuff is chief L VOORMEZEELE.	
	28/9		To supply working party for two field works accommodation for W.O.'s on WP of HOOGENZEZE bath on an O.P. of W.O.'s by RCA O.P. at Dickebusch	EBND.

WAR DIARY
or
INTELLIGENCE SUMMARY.

Army Form C. 2118.

62ND ARMY TROOPS COMPANY, R.E.

SEPT 1918 cont

Place	Date	Hour	Summary of Events and Information	Remarks and references to Appendices
DICKEBUSCH AREA	27		The battle began at 5.30 a.m. The 62nd & 15th Divs began to push to the frontline steadily. Heard the STEOL control began to reinforce the lines.	
			9th of the hill the Engrs on left relay at all ambulances there.	
			Just [illegible] - 5.30 p.m. a 30th & we are [illegible] for [illegible]	
			To WULFBEKE [illegible]	
			evening - 30 [illegible]	

A. Mulhollough, Capt.
OC 62 Army Tp Coy RE

WAR DIARY
or
INTELLIGENCE SUMMARY.
(Erase heading not required.)

Army Form C. 2118.

62ND FIELD COMPANY R.E.

OCTOBER 1915 No. 38

Place	Date	Hour	Summary of Events and Information	Remarks and references to Appendices
WULVERGHEM AREA	27	2 p.m.	The by road from this even to WYTSCHAETE, the transport from further back fell in behind them & the whole moved off together. The enemy shewed in bad officer's planning the WYTSCHAETE × roads, that the transport column got into difficulties in that although there are gate-ways & means round in front we were more than an hour late in leaving the starting point, which was the VIERSTRAAT × roads. The road from FRANS BOIS to WYTSCHAETE was so bad that I decided to leave the transport parked near the VIERSTRAAT × roads taking it on the 2nd nite via YORK RD & so near LINDENHOEK, DAYLIGHT CORNER & WULVERGHEM. The section when in the water cart came on with the Coy. From 02.00 to 13.00 or so there was 8 hours hard work for the Coy from 13.00 fought refugees of the town the accumulation in WYTSCHAETE with cellars crowded the minimum of this whole matter is settled with shell like in considerable numbers of billets shelling officer when cellars & bivouacs made & [illegible] [illegible] [illegible] [illegible] were [illegible] [illegible]	

62nd
F.&D. COMPANY.
R.E.

Army Form C. 2118.

WAR DIARY
or
INTELLIGENCE SUMMARY.

(Erase heading not required.)

OCTOBER 1918

Place	Date	Hour	Summary of Events and Information	Remarks and references to Appendices
WYTSCHAETE	1st		WYTSCHAETE or MESSINES RD. by Wulverghem getting stuck in a narrow bit. [remainder illegible]	
	2nd		[illegible]	
WULVERGHEM	3rd		WULVERGHEM when we made a camp. On the 3rd we began work on the WULVERGHEM – MESSINES RD with 15 ofs & 315 N Labour Corps ratings. No [illegible] it. Starting began a mile behind the front [illegible]	

Army Form C. 2118.

62ND FIELD COMPANY

WAR DIARY
or
INTELLIGENCE SUMMARY.
(Erase heading not required.)

OCTOBER 1918.

Instructions regarding War Diaries and Intelligence Summaries are contained in F. S. Regs., Part II. and the Staff Manual respectively. Title pages will be prepared in manuscript.

Place	Date	Hour	Summary of Events and Information	Remarks and references to Appendices
WULVERGHEM	5th-11th		Men of HESSNES when a road breakdown in the road. Work on MESSINES – WULVERGHEM Road. Bridge erected at 28/U.2.6.5.0. for lorries.	Nil.
Do	12th-14th		Coy standing by. The whole coy bathed.	Nil.
Do	15th		The O.C. with Lt. PRESTON made reconnaissance of Br. Bgr. in COMINES	Nil.
Do			Coy moved to SAILOR'S CROSSING 28/V.2.8.	Nil.
SAILORS Crossing	16th-17th		Bridges erected over LYS at COMINES (28/V.4 central)	Nil.
Do	18th		Coy moved forward to LE BLANC FOUR 28/X.19.6. One section remaining at 28/V.4 central to finish bridge.	Nil.
			Capt R.F. FRYER left Coy to take over duties as O.C. 547th Field Coy R.E.	
LE BLANC FOUR	19th		Coy HQrs. One section moved to MUSCRON. Remaining section moved from 28/V.4. central to LE BLANC FOUR	Nil.
MUSCRON	20th		One Section remained Coy. Coy and transport moved to EVREGNIES. Bridges for lorries erected at 37/B.7.C.8.4. Bridge for 1st line transport stuck at 37/B.18.C.5.9.	Nil.
			1 OFF. & 50 OR's (Austrians) attacked tby.
			Lt. E.V. DEVERALL from 89th Field Coy R.E. joined Coy as 2nd in Command

WAR DIARY
or
INTELLIGENCE SUMMARY.

(Erase heading not required.)

Army Form C. 2118.

62ND FIELD COMPANY R.E.

Place	Date	Hour	Summary of Events and Information	Remarks and references to Appendices
EVREGNIES	21st		Bridges for 1st line transport completed at 37/B17 d.10	Knl.
	22nd		Bridge at 37/B17 d.10 completed. Material for floating bridge taken to ESPIERES from EVREGNIES.	Knl.
do	23rd		Moved to DOTTIGNIES. Lt. PRESTON proceeded to U.K. on leave. Lt. TOBIN with his Section attempted to put bridge across river.	Knl.
DOTTIGNIES	24th		Bridge at B/18 C.5.9. attempted to take lorries. Major J.H. HOLLEY killed in action on the bank of the SCHELD RIVER south east of ESPIERES. Light infy foot bridge constructed on main road across canal at ESPIERES.	Knl.
do	25th		Coy. cleaning up.	Knl.
do	26th		Coy. arrived at ESTAIMPUIS. Constructing bridges at EVREGNIES 37/B9 d.7.1. for 12 Ton Axle load. Capt. L.G.M. LYON from 89th Field Coy. took over command. Lt. W.S. BROWNE to 89th Field Coy RE as 2nd in command	Knl.
ESTAIMPUIS	27th		Completed Bridge at EVREGNIES	Knl.
do	28th		Sections cleaning equipment wagons	Knl.
do	29th		Coy paraded full marching order. Coy & Section drill. Lewis Gun instruction.	Knl.

Army Form C. 2118.

WAR DIARY
or
INTELLIGENCE SUMMARY.

Place	Date	Hour	Summary of Events and Information	Remarks and references to Appendices
ESTAMPUIS	30th		Stores taken up the line so that no time will be wasted when order is given to erect bridges. Coy. parade Box Respirator Drill, Rifle Drill and Lewis Gun instruction. Football in afternoon.	nil.
Do.	31st		Coy. parade. Route March. Lieut. MERCIER investigated mine at HERSEAU. Pontoons & trestle fetched from 61st 2nd Coy. dump as they will be required for bridging when enemy retires.	nil.

Inkpen Capt. RE
O.C. 62nd Field Coy. R.E.
31/1/18.

Army Form C. 2118.

NOVEMBER 1918

62ND FIELD COMPANY R.E.

WAR DIARY
or
INTELLIGENCE SUMMARY.
(Erase heading not required.)

Place	Date	Hour	Summary of Events and Information	Remarks and references to Appendices
ESTAIMPUIS	1/11/18		Company training – Drill Poor Yunsek in morning – Football afternoon. Lecture by Lt Purcell Educatl Offr	
"	2/11/18		Company training as above. Football in afternoon and French class to OR by a both at the Convent.	
"	3/11/18		Route march until 10·30 – Church (voluntary) parade at 11 – Football afternoon and usual French lesson.	
"	4/11/18		Company training in Bridging near Cpl Lawrence's during afternoon. Roofed huts in HERSEAUX searched for.	
"	5/11/18		Check parade in morning – drill training in bridging. Looking up/to afternoon – French class afternoon. Baths HERSEAUX.	
"	6/11/18		Work on R.E. dump at B.38 cent. Lieut W.S. Brand rejoined Coy & proceeded on course to ROUEN same day.	
"	7/11/18		Work on transport party to ROUBAIX for material – HAMILTON ROADWAY and party to DIVISIONAL REST STATION for work at Camp – Capt. H. H. F. RG rejoined 69th Field Coy RE – Major A. Grantham RE joined	

Army Form C. 2118.

WAR DIARY
or
INTELLIGENCE SUMMARY.
(Erase heading not required.)

62ND FIELD COMPANY, R.E.

Place	Date	Hour	Summary of Events and Information	Remarks and references to Appendices
	9/11/18		62nd Field Coy. from 29th Field Coy. RE. — Capt. Deverell M.C. R.E. assumed to H.M. Field Ambulance div. — Coy. moves to DOTTIGNIES — Sheet 37/B.11.b. — Orders received that the enemy had retired & that this Coy. under put a bridge (pontoon) across L'ESCAUT at HELCHIN and build two lorry bridges across the River Espierres and Canal d'Espierres (Sheet 37/C.9.c) at ESPIERRES.	
	10/11/18		Pontoon Bridge was finished at 1500 hours. Bridges at ESPIERRES continued. — A bridge to carry motorised transport was started across the marsh at HELCHIN (Sheet 37/B.6.	
	11/11/18		Bridges at ESPIERRES finished — work on bridge at HELCHIN continued.	
	12/11/18		Bridge at HELCHIN finished. —	
	13/11/18		Company cleaning up and resting.	
	14/11/18		Warning orders received that Coy. would be moving on the 15th	
LA MADELEINE	15/11/18		Company moved to LA MADELEINE — for work under orders CE XV Corps. Attached Croix-Roleau. rejoined Heavy Artillery Which —	
(LILLE)	16/11/18		Coy. went round work to be done with CRE XV Corps Troops —	

WAR DIARY
or
INTELLIGENCE SUMMARY

Army Form C. 2118.

62ND FIELD COMPANY. R.E.

Place	Date	Hour	Summary of Events and Information	Remarks and references to Appendices
	17/11/16		No work – Coy were inspected by O/C. 2 R. Forces proceeded on special leave to UK	
	18/11/16		Work started clearing demolished & reinforced concrete bridge blown by enemy from railway to LILLE (Sheet 36/K 30 a 5.0) – Capt Deverell R.C.R.E. returned Coy from hospital.	
	19/11/16		Work continued. 3 lines now cleared	
	20/11/16		Do. All new iron has been detached & course Iron now repaired	
	21/11/16		Do.	
	22/11/16		Do.	
	23/11/16		Do. 5 lines now cleared	
	24/11/16		No work – Inspection by O/C of Coy in full marching order.	
	25/11/16		Major A Granthow RE proceeded on leave. Capt Deverell MCRE taken over command of Coy. Work continued on Rugford downend Loop which had been dropped on railway. Lines added on Ry wagons and removed by 10th Canadian Railway Bridge	
	26/11/16		Same work continued. Another job of clearing started at 36/K 35 b 4.2 Brick Arch.	

Army Form C. 2118.

WAR DIARY
or
INTELLIGENCE SUMMARY.
(Erase heading not required.)

Place	Date	Hour	Summary of Events and Information	Remarks and references to Appendices
	27/11/18		Both jobs continued and in addition 14 men under a corporal commenced running balow rails, panels etc between the two bridges and making necessary improvements to open the two outside tracks for traffic.	
	28/11/18		Above continued	
	29/11/18		do	
	30/11/18		do	

MacDonnell
Capt RE
A/O.C., 62nd Field Co RE

[Stamp: 62ND FIELD COMPANY. R.E.]

WAR DIARY
or
INTELLIGENCE SUMMARY.
(Erase heading not required.)

Army Form C. 2118.

62ND FIELD COMPANY R.E.

Vol 48

Place	Date	Hour	Summary of Events and Information	Remarks and references to Appendices
LA MADELEINE Sh.36.K21d57	1/7/18	0930	Company paraded for Inspection in Full Marching Order.	
		1115	Pay Parade. In the afternoon a game of football was played between No.1 Section and HQ Section.	
	2/7/18	0745	Company paraded for work. The clearing away of demolished bridge at Sh.36/K35b 4.2 and K30a 5.0. Broken rails and permanent way taken out and replaced, rerailed and sleepers levelled. In the afternoon a football match was played between No.3 and the No.2.	
	3/7/18		Work continued. Football match between No.3 and HQ Sections.	
	4/7/18		Work continued. Sergt. CARR A (R.E.) & Cpl. McMASTER A (R.E.) Awarded French Croix de Guerre. 14 Div. D.R.O. 4/7/18	
	5/7/18		Work continued. 2nd Lieut D.C.C. MERCIER returned from leave in U.K.	
	6/7/18		Work continued. Additional work was undertaken at K24d 5.4	
	7/7/18		No work. Company (Less Maintce) giving 2 hours hard drill, Rifle exercises and Ceremony Drill. In afternoon the whole company turned out to see His Majesty KING GEORGE V who passed along Boulvard from ROUBAIX to LILLE.	

WAR DIARY
INTELLIGENCE SUMMARY.

(Erase heading not required.)

Army Form C. 2118.

62nd FIELD COMPANY R.E.

Place	Date	Hour	Summary of Events and Information	Remarks and references to Appendices
LA MADELEINE SH36/K21d 5.7	8/12/18	09.30	Company paraded in Full Marching Order for Inspection.	
	9/12/18	11.00	Pay Parade and Passes issued for LILLE	
		07.45	Railway reconstruction continued at K.24.d. Broken rails removed and replaced and roadbed repaired.	
	10/12/18		Same work continued. Routine Order 40th Division dated December 4th 1918 received stating that MAJOR A. GRANTHAM R.E. has been awarded CROIX DE GUERRE (Division, with Silver Star)	
	11/12/18		Work continued on Railway.	
	12/12/18		Work continued on Railway. MAJOR A. GRANTHAM R.E. returns from leave and takes over command of Company from Capt. E.V. Severall 2ic RE	
	13/12/18		Work on railways continued. Game played between sections in afternoon.	
	14/12/18		Work as above continued.	
	15/12/18		Company paraded in full marching order for inspection by O.C. Ranks were inspected and men were told a football match was played in the afternoon.	

WAR DIARY or INTELLIGENCE SUMMARY

Army Form C. 2118.

62nd FIELD COMPANY, R.E.

Place	Date	Hour	Summary of Events and Information	Remarks and references to Appendices
LA MADELEINE	16/12/18		Work continued on railway. Work now consisted of relaying points and crossovers and fitting in where other points had been demolished by enemy.	
	17/12/18		Work continued	
	18/12/18		Work continued	
	19/12/18		Work continued. 2nd Lieut. HEYWOOD R.E. joined company from the Base.	
	20/12/18		Work continued	
	21/12/18		Work continued	
	22/12/18		Full marching order parade for inspection. Pay and football.	
	23/12/18		Work continued. One section preparing dining room for the Company Xmas dinner. 2nd Lieut. D.C.C. MERCIER R.E. attached 23rd Lancs Fusiliers for 6 weeks.	
	24/12/18		Work continued. Information received that no more work on railway was necessary.	
	25/12/18		Xmas Day. Dinner for all the men at 17.00 hours and concert followed.	
	26/12/18		Boxing Day. No parade.	

WAR DIARY
or
INTELLIGENCE SUMMARY

Army Form C. 2118.

Place	Date	Hour	Summary of Events and Information	Remarks and references to Appendices
La Madeleine	27/12/18		Coy. paraded 0900 hours squad drill & PT an hour.	
K21A 5.7	28/12/18		Inspection of billets and football. Major A. Grantham R.E. mentioned in despatch Gazette 27/12/18	
	29/12/18		Training on above continued.	
	30/12/18		C.O. marching order parade for inspection. Toy and football. Lieut. C.T. BITT R.E. returns from leave.	
	31/12/18		Training contd. The bad weather interfered considerably with outdoor training.	

[signature] Major RE
O.C. 62nd Field Coy RE
31/12/18

WAR DIARY or INTELLIGENCE SUMMARY

Army Form C. 2118.

JANUARY 1919.

62 4th Coy R.E.

Place	Date	Hour	Summary of Events and Information	Remarks and references to Appendices
LA MADELEINE LILLE SHEET 36 N 21 d 5,7	Jan 1st		The Company was engaged preparing for demobilization. One hours Drill and ½ hours Physical training. 1 O.R. DEMOBILIZED. In the afternoon ½ hours educational training	A.
	2.		Training Continued	A.
	3.		Training Continued. 2 O.R. DEMOBILIZED	A.
	4.		Training Continued	A.
	5.		Parade of whole Company for inspection by the O.C. R. Football match was played in the afternoon	A.
	6.		The Company paraded as usual for drill & physical training	A.
	"		5 REINFORCEMENTS arrived from the Base.	A.
	7.		Erection of 2 huts for 43rd INFY BDE started at BONDUE. 16 O.R. employed. Training as usual. 1 O.R. DEMOBILIZED	A.
	8.		Work on huts at BONDUE & training continued.	A.
	9.		A Committee consisting of 1/Lt J.W. PRESTON R.E. and 3 O.R. proceeded to C.R.E. HQRS re a wreath in reference to the R.E. WAR MEMORIAL. It was decided that Company should subscribe, and it was the Companies	

Army Form C. 2118.

WAR DIARY
or
INTELLIGENCE SUMMARY.
(Erase heading not required.)

Instructions regarding War Diaries and Intelligence Summaries are contained in F. S. Regs., Part II. and the Staff Manual respectively. Title pages will be prepared in manuscript.

62nd FIELD COMPANY, R.E.

Place	Date 1919.	Hour	Summary of Events and Information	Remarks and references to Appendices
LA MADELINE LILLE SHEET 36 K2 Id 5.7	Jan 9		Opinion that the money should go towards the erection of a Building in London to be used as a Club etc. Work on huts at	PJ.
	"		BONDUE and training continued. 1. O.R. DEMOBILIZED.	PJ.
	10		Work on huts and training continued.	PJ.
	11		Work on huts and training continued.	PJ.
	12		Parade of whole Company for inspection by O.C. a football match was played in the afternoon. 5. O.R. DEMOBILIZED.	PJ.
	13		Work on huts and training continued. 3. O.R. DEMOBILIZED.	PJ.
	14		Work on huts and training continued.	PJ.
	15		Work on huts and training continued.	PJ.
	16		Work on huts and training continued.	PJ.
	17		Another hut erected at MARCQ.	PJ.
	18		Work on huts and training continued.	PJ.
	19		Company engaged cleaning up thoroughly all their equipment. 6.O.R. DEMOBILIZED	PJ.
	20		Work and training continued. 6. O.R. DEMOBILIZED. 7. REINFORCEMENTS arrived from the Base.	PJ.

Army Form C. 2118.

62ND FIELD COMPANY, R.E.

WAR DIARY
or
INTELLIGENCE SUMMARY.
(Erase heading not required.)

Instructions regarding War Diaries and Intelligence Summaries are contained in F. S. Regs., Part II. and the Staff Manual respectively. Title pages will be prepared in manuscript.

JANUARY 1919

Place	Date 1919	Hour	Summary of Events and Information	Remarks and references to Appendices
LA MADELEINE LILLE.	JAN. 21.		Work on huts and training continued. 6. O.R. DEMOBILIZED.	A.4
	22		Inspection of the Company by Brigd. General SINGER R.E., CHIEF ENGR. 15TH CORPS. The Chief Engineer expressed his pleasure with the turn out of the whole Company. 3 O.R. DEMOBILIZED	A.4
	23		Work on huts and training continued. LONDON GAZETTE JANy 20TH 1919. No 40095 published the Award of the M.S.M. to No. 5073 CARR. T. and Sgt. No. 60182 EDWARDS of this Company.	A.4
	24		Work on huts and training continued.	A.4
	25		Work on huts and training continued.	A.4
	26		Inspection of Section by Section Officers. 5. O.R. DEMOBILIZED. 2 REINFORCEMENTS arrived from Base.	A.4
	27		Work on huts and training continued. 5. OR DEMOBILIZED.	A.4
	28		Work on huts and training continued. 11. OR DEMOBILIZED. Strength of the Company. EFFECTIVE 123 O.R's and 6 Officers. RATION STRTH 100 O.R's and 4 Officers	A.4
	29.		Work on huts & various Training continued 10 O.R. DEMOBILIZED.	A.4

Army Form C. 2118.

62ND FIELD COMPANY R.E.

JANUARY 1919.

WAR DIARY
or
INTELLIGENCE SUMMARY.
(Erase heading not required.)

Instructions regarding War Diaries and Intelligence Summaries are contained in F. S. Regs., Part II. and the Staff Manual respectively. Title pages will be prepared in manuscript.

Place	Date 1919	Hour	Summary of Events and Information	Remarks and references to Appendices
LA MADELINE LILLE	Jan 30		Training as usual continued. All stores and equipment of company checked. Horses of the coy. were mallused preparatory to demobilization.	P.7.
	" 31		Training as usual continued.	P.1.

MAJOR, R.E.
COMMANDING 62nd FIELD COMPANY R.E.

WAR DIARY
INTELLIGENCE SUMMARY

Army Form C. 2118.

62ND FIELD COMPANY R.E.

FEBRUARY 1919.

Place	Date	Hour	Summary of Events and Information	Remarks and references to Appendices
LA MADELEINE LILLE SHEET 36 K21 d 57	FEB 1st		The company was still engaged preparing for demobilization. The effective strength of unit on this date was 6 officers 121 O.R. The week was being done by the Company, except drill and recreational training.	R.I.
	2nd		Inspection of company in full marching order by O.C. 10 O.R. were demobilized. Lieut C.R. TANT, R.E. left unit to be attached to the Staff of the Animal Demobilizing Camp at TOURCOING.	R.I.
	3rd		3 O.R. demobilized.	R.I.
	4th		The demobilization of the horses commenced. 6 were sent to LINSELLES.	R.I.
	5th		Training as usual.	R.I.
	6th		CAPT. E.V. DEVERALL, R.E. returned from leave to U.K. 6 O.R. demobilized.	R.I.
	7th		1 O.R. demobilized	R.I.
	8th		A list of names of O.R. compulsorily retained under ARMY ORDER XIV for Armies of Occupation was published showing 17 O.R. and 7 O.R. unexpired Colour Service, making a total of 19 O.R.	R.I.
	9th		Inspection of company in full marching order by the O.C. 5 O.R. demobilized.	R.I.

Army Form C. 2118.

62ND FIELD COMPANY. R.E.
No.
Date.

WAR DIARY
or
INTELLIGENCE SUMMARY.
(Erase heading not required.)

FEBRUARY 1919

Place	Date	Hour	Summary of Events and Information	Remarks and references to Appendices
LA MADELEINE LILLE	FEB 10th		Training &c. continued. 3 O.R. demobilized.	A.Y.
	" 11th		do.	A.Y.
	" 12th		do.	A.Y.
	" 13th		do.	A.Y.
	" 14th		do. 3 O.R. demobilized.	A.Y.
	" 15th		do. The ration strength of the unit at this date is only 5 officers and 69 O.R.	A.Y.
	" 16th		Inspection of Company and of all billets &c by the O.C.	A.Y.
	" 17th		Training &c. continued. 2 O.R. demobilized.	A.Y.
	" 18th		4 O.R. (Sappers) were attached to 61st Field Coy R.E. These men were retained for Army of Occupation, and were to reinforce Field Coys. of the 34TH DIVN.	A.Y.
	" 19th		Training &c. continued.	A.Y.
	" 20th		do.	A.Y.
	" 21st		do. 2 O.R. demobilized.	A.Y.
	" 22nd		do.	A.Y.

WAR DIARY
INTELLIGENCE SUMMARY

62ND FIELD COMPANY R.E.

FEBRUARY 1919

Place	Date	Hour	Summary of Events and Information	Remarks and references to Appendices
MARKEINE	FEB. 23rd		Kit inspection. The strength of the unit on this date is 5 officers and 63 O.R. to which Reinf. of Occupation cannot be included in Colar of that deficiency of 15 O.R. that is continued in Colar. (which is 65 O.R.)	R.E.
	24th		do.	R.E.
	25th		do.	R.E.
	26th		do.	R.E.
	27th		do.	R.E.
	28th		do.	R.E.

B. Moulton (Major R.E.)
O.C. 62nd Field Coy R.E.

WAR DIARY
or
INTELLIGENCE SUMMARY.
(Erase heading not required.)

Army Form C. 2118.

622nd FIELD COMPANY. R.E.

Vol 43

Place	Date	Hour	Summary of Events and Information	Remarks and references to Appendices
LA MADELEINE LILLE	MAR 1st		The Company was preparing for demobilization. The effective strength on this date was 6 Officers and 81 O.R.	
	2nd		Inspection of Coy. in full marching order by O.C.	
	3rd		Training etc. carried on	
	4th		- do -	
	5th		- do - Orders were received for Company to move to HERSEAUX BELGIUM	
	6th		- do - Company made preparations for move	
	7th		Company moved to HERSEAUX (BELGIUM) but owing to Company horses being demobilized move could not be completed in one journey. Only 26 horses & mules were available.	
	8th		The move to HERSEAUX was completed	
HERSEAUX (BELGIUM)	9th		The Company worked under C.S.M. making huts comfortable.	
	10th		- do -	
	11th		20 Corporals were demobilized 10 to WIMILLES and 10 to TOURCOING billeting Coys.	
	12th		Company worked under C.S.M.	
	13th		- do -	

Army Form C. 2118.

62ND FIELD COMPANY, R.E.

WAR DIARY
or
INTELLIGENCE SUMMARY

(Erase heading not required.)

Instructions regarding War Diaries and Intelligence Summaries are contained in F. S. Regs., Part II. and the Staff Manual respectively. Title pages will be prepared in manuscript.

MARCH 1919 Continued

Place	Date	Hour	Summary of Events and Information	Remarks and references to Appendices
HERSEAUX BELGIUM	MARCH			
	15th		Company training etc. Effective strength at this date 5 officers + 75 O.R. Orders were received from CRE that O/Major GROTHAM, LIEUT BROWNE and Lieut PRESTON would be transferred to 483rd FIELD COY 2nd DIVISION. This move to be carried out at once. These officers were volunteers for ARMY of the RHINE.	
	16th		LIEUT BROWNE was on leave and would follow up later. The Cadre Coy was to be known by ✗ Capt RICHMOND from 61st Field Coy R.E.	
	17th		Training etc. as usual.	
	18th		—do—	
	19th		7 Animals demobilized to TOURCOING Collecting Camp. Orders received that all returnable personnel were to be transferred to 231st FIELD COY.	
	20th		13 O.R. were transferred to 231st Field Coy.	
	21st		Company at usual work	
	22nd		Actual strength of Company 3 Officers + 48 O.R. LIEUT BROWNE returned from leave. 5 horses demobilized to Lunelles Collecting Camp. Training etc continued	
	23rd			
	24th		LIEUT BROWNE proceeded to join the 483rd FIELD COY. 2 Horses demobilized to TOURCOING	
	25th		Training etc continued. No animals with company now	

(19175) Wt W3358/P3560 600,000 12/17 D. D. & L. **Sch. 52a.** Forms/C2118/5.

WAR DIARY

INTELLIGENCE SUMMARY

Army Form C. 2118.

62ND FIELD COMPANY, R.E.

Place	Date	Hour	Summary of Events and Information	Remarks and references to Appendices
HERSEAUX. (BELGIUM)	MAR 26th		Training as usual.	
	27		— do —	
	28		— do — 3 O.R. provided for demobilisation	
	29th		— do —	
	30th		— do —	
	31st		— do — The effective strength went 2 Officers 55 O.R.	

E.A.A. Kirkwood Capt.
MAJOR, R.E.
COMMANDING 62nd FIELD COMPANY R.E.

WAR DIARY
or
INTELLIGENCE SUMMARY.
(Erase heading not required.)

Army Form C. 2118.

62nd Coy R.E.

Place	Date	Hour	Summary of Events and Information	Remarks and references to Appendices
HERSEAUX. (BAGIUM)	1.4.19 to 15.4.19		Coy reduced to 40 all ranks. In works other than camp maintenance being carried out	
	15.4.19		Considerable number of complaints from men in the Coy about the slowness of demobilization these I passed to CRE.	
	16.4.19		The XV Corps Commander Brig-Gen. LEVESON-GOWER C.M.G. D.S.O. inspected the Coy. I interviewed all those men having complaints to make. Notes on these cases forwarded to Division	
	16.4.19		Capt F.D. Richmond the C.O. of 7th Coy Coy proceeded on leave, all other officers of the company were subsequently transferred to the RHINE ARMY. Capt L.G.M. LYON R.E. took over command also Capt Richmond was transferred to command of the 61 Field Coy R.E. with effect from that Capt L.G.M. LYON R.E. proceeded on leave. Major S. SNE G R.E. 61 FDCy taking over command of the Coy. Nothing on subsequent days to record	
	30.4.19		Party of 4 ORs proceeded on a trip to BRUGES, & to RHINE.	

L.G.M. Lyon
Major
O.C. 62nd

42nd Inf Bde Group

    Herewith War Diary of this unit for month of May please.

2/6/19

                                     Capt, R.E.
            COMMANDING 62nd FIELD COMPANY R.E.

WAR DIARY
or
INTELLIGENCE SUMMARY.
(Erase heading not required.)

Army Form C. 2118.

62ND FIELD COMPANY, R.E.

No. ....
Date 1/6 46

Place	Date	Hour	Summary of Events and Information	Remarks and references to Appendices
HERSEAUX (Belgium)	1.5.19		Coy reduced to 40 O.R. Men employed on Coy. fatigues. No important work being carried out.	
	31.5.19		Capt. Lyon returned from leave on the 6th.	Nil.

Lyon Capt. R.E.
MAJOR, R.E.
COMMANDING 62nd FIELD COMPANY R.E.

Army Form C. 2118.

62ND FIELD COMPANY. R.E.

No. ....
Date ....

WAR DIARY
or
INTELLIGENCE SUMMARY.
(Erase heading not required.)

Place	Date	Hour	Summary of Events and Information	Remarks and references to Appendices
HERSEAUX	1.6.19		Strength of Coy reduced to 40 O.R's	
	6.6.19		Cadre of Coy left for demobilisation, strength reduced to 13 O.R. 5O. These were kept for guarding transport sta.	
	16.6.19		Transport guard left HERSEAUX Sta. for U.K.	

Lindsay, Capt R.E.
O.C. 62nd Fd Coy R.E.

www.ingramcontent.com/pod-product-compliance
Lightning Source LLC
Chambersburg PA
CBHW081400160426
43193CB00013B/2075